MW01115569

CALLED CHRISTIANS

Billy B. Dunbar

ISBN 978-1-0980-9448-5 (paperback)
ISBN 978-1-0980-9449-2 (digital)

Christian Faith Publishing, Inc.
832 Park Avenue
Meadville, PA 16335
www.christianfaithpublishing.com

Printed in the United States of America

INTRODUCTION

> And the disciples were called Christians first in Antioch.
>
> —Acts 11:26

When this verse caught my attention, my initial response was to prepare a sermon. In the process of doing so, I quickly discovered the ideas were not coming together rapidly and harmoniously into a well-rounded message.

Occasionally, a sermon comes as easily as the heavenly manna that fell overnight for the children of Israel. Most, however, require diligent study and research. A few are constructed piecemeal with inspiration and revelation coming in small degrees over a long period of time. This sermon from Acts 11:26 was a piecemeal construction. But after preparing two different sermons from this text, I still found myself intrigued by two words: *called Christians.*

This verse is the only place the word *Christians* appears in the Bible. The singular form of the word is used only twice (1 Peter 4:16, Acts 26:28). In both the church and the world, the word *Christian(s)*, whether singular or plural, is used somewhat loosely these days.

This reference is also the first time believers were identified by the title "Christian." Until this time, they had no recognized name. Why was the title given in Antioch? Many scholars believe the name was given to mock those who voiced their faith in Christ. Others believe it was given by the Gentile population at Antioch as a title of distinction. Most agree the name was not given by the Jews, for to do so would be to admit that Christ was the *Messiah*. Whatever the reason and whoever is responsible, the name given to the "disciples," or followers of Christ, the anointed one, remains today.

Disciples are commonly identified after the name of their leader—for example, Buddhists, Wesleyans, etc. Something about the lifestyle of the disciples reminded others of Christ. Therefore, they were called by His name; in other words, they were named after Him. The evidence of Christlikeness was apparent before the name was applied.

What an honor to be called "Christians!" Although originally, the name was perhaps meant as mockery and a mark of dishonor, it now distinguishes us as being in the Savior and the Savior in us. The designation "Christian" carries with it certain responsibilities and obligations. It is incumbent we walk worthy of that honorable name by departing from iniquity (2 Timothy 2:19) by walking in Christ's steps (1 Peter 2:21, 1 John 2:6) and by continuing His message (Matthew 28:18–20).

Perhaps no other verse paints a better portrait of Christ than does Acts 10:38: "How God anointed Jesus of Nazareth with the Holy Ghost and with power: who went about doing good, and healing all that were oppressed of the devil; for God was with him." Being anointed with the Holy Ghost and power *and* doing good are marks of a true Christian.

After spending many hours in prayerful meditation and research, I have divided my thoughts about Acts 11:26 into two mainstreams. Both areas are stimulated by questions about the phrase "called Christians."

"Are all who are called Christians truly Christians indeed, or are they just 'called' Christians?"

We must realize that what we are called does not determine our eternal destiny but rather what we *are*. Chapters 1–3 describe three types of people who are called Christians but whose relationship with Christ is questioned in Scripture. The fourth chapter presents a type of Christian who has gone the extra mile to ensure his eternal future with God (see 2 Peter 1:10).

"Why were they called Christians first at this particular location, Antioch, after the church had been in existence approximately ten years?"

This question led to a study of the Antioch Church where the name originated. The Antioch Church was planted by men from the church at Jerusalem, which had been started by men who had been with Christ. It stands to reason the apostles were Christlike when they established the early church at Jerusalem. It also stands to reason the men who went out from Jerusalem to pioneer the church at Antioch followed their example and were given that beautiful name by which we are still called today.

Chapters 5–9 deal with the Antioch example, with each chapter detailing a characteristic that could be seen both in the church at Jerusalem and in the life of Christ.

I hope a divinely given mixture of affection, wisdom, and firmness is found in this work. My purpose is to help all of us to live up to that name by which we are called so we will be ready at Christ's return.

SECTION 1

These chapters deal with professing Christianity in the contemporary church. Examples show the reality of the present. Some individuals are truly Christlike, others provoke questions about just how closely they exemplify Christ in their lifestyle. Using the Word of God as a guide, determine what characteristics are reflected in your lifestyle.

CHAPTER 1

Cotton Candy Christians

Some professing Christians appear on the surface to be vibrant, excited, and appealing, but like beautiful multicolored balloons under the aim of an accurate dart thrower, they quickly become deflated. They are like cotton candy, which appears beautiful and enormous but dissipates almost instantly when placed in the mouth. Cotton candy is also sweet to the taste, and the sugar gives a burst of energy. However, the sweetness soon leaves a sour aftertaste, and the energy is quickly gone.

So it is with some who are called Christians. They perform well until confronted with the fiery darts and devouring mouth of Satan. Then they discover either the foundational strength or weakness of their Christian experience. Each believer should ask, "What is the true substance of my relationship with Christ? What is the basis for my strength?"

Poor Spiritual Nourishment

Cotton candy Christians like only the sweet, smooth, good times, the mountaintop experiences. But their "high" is of short duration, for they lack a well-balanced diet in things pertaining to the Christian life. They could learn a good lesson from observing children.

When allowed to do so, young children will neglect three well-balanced meals a day in favor of a diet loaded with sugar. After consuming cookies, candy, Cokes, and Kool-Aid, they become energetic, even hyperactive, but this excessive energy is short-lived. They must return often to the refrigerator or cookie jar to maintain this high-energy level. What they don't realize is that three solid meals a day will give them more consistent energy even though the food may not be as appealing to their taste buds as the sweets.

The same is true of cotton candy Christians. They are full of energy when there is a great outpouring of the Holy Spirit with physical manifestations. Such blessings from God certainly should excite believers, but cotton candy Christians run out of steam when attacked by the enemy. When smooth sailing ends and their ship is tempest-tossed, they are soon removed from dancing on the mountain to dragging in the valley.

An ounce of prevention *is* worth a pound of cure as the adage says. This yo-yo experience can be prevented by application of the simple fundamentals of the Christian life: consistent and unhurried daily prayer, consistent daily reading of God's Word through a slow and meditative process, consistent church attendance, and keeping company with believers who serve God faithfully day in and day out, regardless of their situation.

Infertile and Uncultivated Soil

Cotton candy believers possibly, even probably, begin their Christian journey on the wrong path. They resemble the stony-ground hearer in the Parable of the Sower. Jesus said, "Some fell on stony ground, where it had not much earth; and immediately it sprang up because it had no depth of earth: But when the sun was up, it was scorched; and because it had no root, it withered away" (Mark 4:5–6).

In explaining the parable, Jesus said, "And these are they likewise which are sown on stony ground who, when they have heard the Word, immediately receive it with gladness and have no root in themselves and so endure but for a time: afterward, when affliction or persecution ariseth for the Word's sake, immediately they are offended" (Mark 4:16–17).

In no way does Scripture lead us to believe the life of a child of God will always be sweet, smooth, and without storms. Jesus said, "In the world ye shall have tribulation" (John 16:33). Paul added, "All that will live godly in Christ Jesus shall suffer persecution" (2 Timothy 3:12). The Bible makes clear there will be difficulties; but with every warning, the Word of God follows with words of hope and encouragement. For example, Jesus continued in John 16:33, "Be of good cheer; I have overcome the world." Paul explained in his letter that Timothy's hope was in continuing in the Scriptures (2 Timothy 3:14–17).

Indeed, the Christian life is one of "joy unspeakable" and "peace which passeth all understanding." However, believers who are not deep-rooted are unaware that this indescribable joy and incomprehensible peace are of a constant nature and are only realized through tests and trials. The enlightenment of this fact will help them become rooted and grounded in the faith. They will learn to endure the bitter while enjoying the sweet.

Feelings Before Faith

Another characteristic of believers who like only sweets is an attitude of emotion for the moment. People with this attitude live for the present without thinking about eternity. Their perception of walking with God will never move past being just an experience into an ongoing relationship with the Lord unless they allow their eyes of understanding to be opened. Emotional highs come and go, but God and His Word remain constant.

For various reasons, some believers seek only temporal excitement. Often, such believers need to appease a guilty conscience because too much time has passed since their last mountaintop experience. In some instances, such people only attend church when they need a so-called "blessing" or, as is sometimes said, "to get their cup filled." When their cup is empty and their blessing has worn off, they begin to feel a void, an emptiness, a sense of guilt. They base much of their Christian experience on feelings. Therefore, when this empty, guilty feeling surfaces, they begin searching for another "spiritual high" to relieve their guilt. Once again, they are like a child returning for a sugar-induced burst of energy.

Another reason these believers are inconsistent is that their focus is in the wrong area. For instance, some quickly get excited over a particular preacher; they begin to look to the man instead of to God. They become captivated by his personality, speech, movements, or other characteristics that stimulate their emotions. The preacher becomes the object of their adoration and the sweet taste that temporarily satisfies their carnal desires. Since this is a carnal substitute, however, it will not sustain them. Once they are out of this person's charming presence, they become deflated and once again in search of another mountaintop.

Still another identifying mark of cotton candy Christians is their tendency to prefer worship services characterized by an upbeat pace and high volume. They do not find fulfillment in teaching sessions or Bible study groups where Scripture is quietly discussed. They have difficulty worshiping when slow, soft choruses that glorify God are sung. They only get involved in worship when the music is loud and lively, and the preaching is fiery. Thank God for such services, but a so-called "lively" (spiritual) service is not always a sign the flock is being fed.

A story about a farmer's hogs and a woodpecker illustrates this. According to the story, when the old farmer went out to feed his hogs, he always pecked on the hog trough before pouring leftover food scraps from the bucket into the trough. When the hogs heard the pecking, they knew it was time to eat and came running in that direction.

A woodpecker observed the process one day and decided to have a little fun with the hogs. He flew to the opposite side of the hogpen and pecked on the fence post. All the hogs went running in that direction. While they were running toward the pecking sound, the woodpecker flew to the other side where the hogs had just come from and pecked on another fence post. Hearing the peck-peck-peck, the hogs came running, but the woodpecker went flying back to the other side and pecked on the fence post. This process continued for quite some time, and the hogs ran off ten to fifteen pounds. Guess what? Those old hogs never did get fed; they were just running after a noise!

We must take heed not to get caught up in running after noise—unless, of course, God is in the noise. The important thing is to distinguish whether or not the noise is authentic.

Elijah had to make that distinction (1 Kings 19). He heard the rustling of the wind, the roaring of the fire, the rumbling of an earthquake, and a still small voice. The first three sounds were much more dramatic than the last. Elijah had previously recognized God in the fire and the rain because he had prayed both down from heaven. This time, however, God was not in the wind, the earthquake, or the fire; rather, He had important instructions for His prophet in a still small voice.

The believer who runs only after the noise has difficulty realizing that in many instances God is in the peacefulness, the calmness, the serenity of the still small voice.

Deficiency without Determination

The characteristics of cotton candy Christians can be traced to a central deficiency—lack of determination. They want to enjoy all the benefits of a follower of Christ without meeting the requirements of cross-bearing and self-denial. They want to reap of the Spirit while sowing to the flesh. Believers are to be "stedfast, unmoveable, always abounding in the work of the Lord," for their "labor is not vain in the Lord" (1 Corinthians 15:58).

Clearly, serving the Lord offers many benefits, but we must realize some labor is involved as well. Being continually active in the work of the Lord requires determination. The sooner we learn this, the more stable we will become as Christians. We should adopt the attitude of the chief apostle: "For I determined not to know anything among you, save Jesus Christ, and him crucified" (1 Corinthians 2:2). With this determination, believers should consistently pray, study God's Word, assemble with other believers, and stedfastly serve God no matter what a day may bring.

CHAPTER 2

Cholesterol Christians

As evangelical Christians, we believe we are saved from sin through and by the blood of Jesus Christ, which was shed on the cross of Calvary. This doctrine is scripturally sound. Colossians 1:20 speaks of making "peace through the blood of his cross." Hebrews 9:22 states, "Without shedding of blood is no remission." According to 1 Peter 1:18–19, believers have been "redeemed with the precious blood of Christ," and 1 John 1:7 records that "the blood of Jesus Christ cleanseth us from all sin." Clearly, the blood is necessary for the remission and cleansing of sin, for making peace with God, and for the redemption of the soul.

> A familiar hymn addresses salvation through the blood:
>
> There is a fountain filled with blood,
> Drawn from Immanuel's veins,
> And sinners plunged beneath that flood,
> Lose all their guilty stains.

This spiritual fountain must be given a free and continuous flow, not only at the outset of salvation but throughout a Christian's life. When the blood is applied, the Holy Spirit takes up residence in us. The "law of the Spirit of life in Christ Jesus" goes into effect and makes individuals "free from the law of sin and death" (Romans 8:2). The blood of Jesus gives us boldness to enter the holiest place

(Hebrews 10:19). By the blood, we are made near to God (Ephesians 2:13).

History has proven that churches who no longer view the blood as significant, relevant, and important, and who have removed the blood from their doctrine are the fastest dying churches. The reason is this: "For the life of the flesh is in the blood" (Leviticus 17:11).

Some three thousand years after this was written, English physician William Harvey discovered in 1628 that blood circulates through the body. The same scripture also says, "For it is the blood that maketh an atonement for the soul." Our spiritual life is in the blood of Jesus, thus the reason churches who no longer propagate this doctrine die spiritually. However, propagation of the value of the blood as a doctrinal belief is not enough. Individuals, as well as churches, who do not keep spiritual channels open to the flow of Jesus Christ in their lives become lethargic in their relationship with Christ. Spiritual application of this medical fact provides helpful insight.

Arteriosclerosis, better known as hardening of the arteries, is a disease in the human body that results in decreased blood flow caused by a narrowing of blood vessels. This narrowing occurs when high levels of cholesterol, a fatty substance, cause fatty deposits on the inner walls of blood vessels. The decreased blood flow results in a decreased supply of oxygen. One of the most effective ways, both to prevent and treat this disease, is to exercise regularly.

Some who are called Christians seem to have a decreased supply of the breath of the Holy Spirit because of a decreased presence of Christ, the lifeblood of the believer, in their lives. Why the decrease? Because the Word of God is not acted upon, not exercised properly in their lives. They become cholesterol Christians.

Hearers, Not Doers

Cholesterol Christians readily absorb the Word of God, but they do not practice it in their daily lives, neither do they see the necessity of spreading the good news or sharing with others the knowledge they have gained. These Christians listen to inspirational tapes and attend Bible seminars, seeming always to want to acquire more knowledge. They are to be commended for their zeal. However, such essential spiritual exercises, as obeying the command to be witnesses of Christ and digging into the God's Word through self-study, prayer, and fasting, are neglected.

The cholesterol Christian is a hearer, not a doer, of the Word. God warned Ezekiel of such people in his congregation:

> And they come unto thee as the people cometh, and they sit before thee as my people, and they hear thy words, but they will not do them: for with their mouth they show much love, but their heart goeth after their covetousness. And lo, thou art unto them as a very lovely song of one that hath a pleasant voice and can play well on an instrument: for they hear thy words, but they do them not.
>
> —Ezekiel 33:31–32

James 1:22 instructs, "But be ye doers of the word, and not hearers only, deceiving your own selves." How terrible it is to be deceived by a friend or by the adversary, but how much more terrible it is to be deceived by oneself! Yet this is what happens to those who absorb the Word but never put it into action. They become spiritually sluggish. Like a sponge soaked with water but not wrung out, they become heavy. The Word of God must be put to use. It is "strong meat" that is profitable when put to use: "But strong meat belongeth to them that are of full age, even those who, by reason of use, have their senses exercised to discern both good and evil" (Hebrews 5:14). The Word must be "mixed with faith" or put into action (exercised) by its hearers to be profitable (see Hebrews 4:2).

Receivers, yet Givers

The Word of God in our lives, Christ in our lives, the Spirit of God in our lives must not be imprisoned within us but must be allowed to flow from us to a hurting world that needs to hear the good news! Consider this: A pond or swamp that always takes in the rains but never gives off becomes stagnant and builds up scum and slime. Likewise, cholesterol Christians who are always taking in the things of God but never give become spiritually stagnant. Consider also the Old Testament manna, which was a type of the Word of God. When not used, it spoiled; "it bred worms, and stank" (Exodus 16:20).

Those who are called Christians should be like a clear flowing stream, which receives the rains and flows through various tributaries to many places. Jesus said, "Freely ye have received, freely give" (Matthew 10:8). God's people must tear down the dams that Satan's subtle beavers are always attempting to build to stop the flow of God. The Church is the channel through which God must flow to bring healing to a hurting world.

The Church is in danger of becoming complacent, "at ease in Zion," as complacent as the Laodicean Church in Revelation 3. The church at Laodicea, according to their own evaluation, was rich and needed nothing. Jesus, however, said they were spiritually blind. When the Church becomes lukewarm and unconcerned and loses its vision of reaching out to those who need a helping hand, it has become spiritually blind.

The same is true of any individual who is called Christian. When Christ abides in our heart, we always need to share Christ with others. Although our contribution to kingdom service may seem small, if done with the right motive, it is eternally significant.

An elderly blind gentleman is a good example of one who seemingly had little reason, resources, or opportunity to help others but who constantly shared the love of God. This eighty-six-year-old gentleman had been totally blind for fifteen years. He was physically feeble and lived alone. Nevertheless, in spite of life's setbacks, he shared the love of God with home-health nurses, social workers, and other visitors who came to his home. He lived next door to a church, and the pastor says he received more when visiting the gentleman than he gave to him. After the pastor visited the sick in hospitals and nursing homes and dealt with oppressing situations, visiting the old blind man and hearing his positive attitude and outlook on life was a welcome reprieve. The old gentleman never mentioned his handicap; instead, he constantly talked of how good God had been to him.

Not only did he share the goodness of God, the old gentleman firmly believed in supporting the work of God with his temporal means despite meager income and resources. He stood on what Jesus said and practiced it. He believed he had received freely of God in all areas of life, and he gave freely. He enjoyed talking about the Scriptures, and although he did not always quote verses verbatim, he did not change their meaning. One of his favorite paraphrased verses—"It's better to give than take"—perhaps summarizes in a nutshell the general purpose of this chapter on the cholesterol Christian.

Action as a Response

Some characters in Scripture help to illustrate the need to act after having received from God. After having received deliverance, the demoniac of Gadara wanted to accompany Jesus. No doubt, he wanted just to observe Christ and absorb more blessings, but Christ said, "Go home to thy friends, and tell them how great things the Lord hath done for thee" (Mark 5:19). If he had continued to observe and absorb the works and blessings of Christ, he would have been of no value to anyone. This miraculous deliverance of such magnitude would have been worth very little if others did not hear of the love, compassion, and power of Christ. Mark 5:20 says, "And he departed and began to publish in Decapolis how great things Jesus had done for him: and all men did marvel." Christ received glory by the man's actions. He received from Christ, and he gave of Christ to others. He did not just hear what Christ said to do, he also did what Christ said to do.

Queen Esther was tempted at first to remain in the safe, comfortable place God had provided for her. This has been the case of all Christians at some period in their Christian life. The intelligent approach seems to be this: If life is smooth sailing, don't rock the boat or even cause a ripple. God, however, has a plan of action for each life. Esther had to be reminded, encouraged, and even admonished by Mordecai. He told her she could very well have been placed where she was in order to deliver her people. He also told her if she did not pursue a course of action, she would be destroyed, and deliverance would come from elsewhere.

This should serve as a reminder that God's Church will continue even though some do not perform their duties and that each individual will be accountable for his actions. Sometimes Christians need both to be reminded of their duty and to remind others to stir up the gift of God that is within them. Esther knew what she had to do, and she did it. Esther's action required the courage to say, "If I perish, I perish." She did not remain in her comfort zone until she became stagnant. By her courageous action, she preserved and delivered her people.

Sometimes believers need the same kind of prodding Mordecai administered to Esther, and other times, just a reminder from God will move them into action. However, one individual in Scripture did not need to be coaxed into action. Joshua had learned much by observing Moses. The time came for him to use the knowledge he had absorbed since God wanted Joshua to be Moses's successor and lead his people, Israel. Joshua responded in active obedience.

Perhaps no other character in the Bible was quicker to respond to God's command. His predecessor, Moses, certainly had quite a dialogue with God before responding. Great prophets like Jeremiah and Isaiah made excuses before answering the call. Joshua, however, immediately began to carry out God's plan.

All believers have the tendency to want to observe and absorb Christ's blessings as the demoniac did. They also tend to want to stay where the spiritual climate is comfortable as Esther did. Both the demoniac and Esther were eventually obedient. However, the best course of action is to obey immediately as Joshua did.

Sadly, some in Scripture did not do their spiritual exercises regularly. One such person was Eli the priest (1 Samuel 1–4). Eli knew what his duties were, but he did not perform them efficiently. He became old and heavy (sluggish) with poor eyesight and poor discernment. Under his leadership, the Word of God became scarce to the Israelites.

Does this type of Christian today realize the eternal significance of obeying God's Word? Or, like Eli, have some become sluggish with poor vision and little discernment, knowing what the Word says but not performing it? What effect will this have on the next generation? Will they take the Word of God seriously if they do not see the previous generation doing so? How long and how many generations before there will be a generation that does not know the Lord? These are important questions for consideration.

When an individual comes to the time when all the secrets of the heart are manifested, it will not matter that he was called a Christian but that he *lived* a Christlike life of obedience to God, both in word and deed. The only issue that will matter is whether or not he acted upon God's Word. Jesus said, "The word that I have spoken, the same shall judge him in the last day" (John 12:48).

The Exercise of Obedience

Just as exercise is effective in treating and preventing cholesterol buildup in the body, so spiritual exercise is an effective way to prevent Christians from becoming spiritually sluggish. We may exercise by obediently applying the principles of God's Word to our daily life and by sharing with others what we have received from God. The Church must arise and be about the Father's business. The Church must ask as did the four lepers, "Why sit we here until we die?" (2 Kings 7:3). The body of Christ must hear Christ say, "Why stand ye here all the day idle? Go ye into the vineyard" (Matthew 20:6–7). The Church must hear what Jesus said: "If ye know these things, happy are ye if ye do them" (John 13:17). May those who are called Christians never forget the words of James: "Therefore to him that knoweth to do good, and doeth it not, to him it is sin" (4:17).

CHAPTER 3

Country-Club Christians

A Christian cannot be a recluse and at the same time serve God as set forth in the Bible. Providing for family and fulfilling the command to be witnesses place Christians in the world. However, God's people must be apart from the world. Jesus said, "They are not of the world even as I am not of the world" (John 17:16).

One of the saddest facts in Christianity is that some who are called Christians possess a seemingly insatiable hunger to impress the world, to win the approval of the world, to be identified with the world. Such individuals stand on the threshold of being conformed to the world, which is forbidden by the Word of God (Romans 12:2). This desire for society's acceptance results in a fence-straddling life-style for which the name country-club Christian is appropriate.

The classification "country-club Christian" does not, in any way, imply that Christians who enjoy a few rounds of golf, a game of tennis, or any other sports activities have stepped outside the boundaries of Scripture as some believe and teach. Our bodies are the temple, the dwelling place, of God. Therefore, considerable attention and physical exercise are necessary to maintain the health of the body. Of course, believers must have their priorities in order, and extracurricular activities must be secondary to their times of communion with God.

The notion that a country club denotes a throng of sports enthusiasts has nothing to do with the type of Christian discussed in this chapter. A person can be a member of a country club and enjoy all the recreational facilities and still not be a country-club Christian.

On the other hand, a person may never have been on the premises of a country club and still fit this description.

Social Acceptance

This concept of the country-club Christian stems from the image of social acceptance and prosperity and prestige in the world a country club projects. Believers should be recognized because Christ can be seen in them, but they should not allow pride or ego to place them under the bondage of peer pressure to receive the world's acclaim and to be like the world. Romans 12:2 admonishes, "Be not conformed to this world." The *Phillips* translation says, "Don't let the world around squeeze you into its own mold."

Just what is meant by the term *world*? The world system in Scripture is that carnal system influenced by Satan and contrary to God. We cannot cater to a fleshly system controlled by Satan and still please a holy God. "They that are in the flesh cannot please God" (Romans 8:8). Jesus said, "No man can serve two masters" (Matthew 6:24). It is vital that every believer see the futility of courting the favor of the world and make a total commitment to God. Romans 8:6 states the consequences of either of the two choices: "For to be carnally minded is death; but to be spiritually minded is life and peace." Perhaps a better understanding of the country-club Christian will help believers who find themselves in the entanglements of the world to separate themselves (2 Corinthians 6:17).

Divided Allegiance

Country-club Christians want the benefits of both the world and the church: "They want their cake and want to eat it too." They want the pleasures, power, popularity, and position of the world system. At the same time, they want the sanctuary, security, satisfaction, and social standing the church has to offer. Their life is a paradox: They want to live as if this is the only world in which they will ever exist, while at the same time, they want the promise and security of living eternally in the world to come. They want eternal life without crucifying the flesh with its affections and lusts (Galatians 5:24). But they cannot have it both ways; they must sell out completely to Christ to have eternal life.

These Christians have never properly cultivated the soil of their heart to receive the Word of God when it is sown. Such people are thorny-ground hearers. Jesus explains this in Mark 4:18–19: "And these are they which are sown among thorns, such as hear the word, and the cares of this world, and the deceitfulness of riches, and the lust of other things entering in, choke the word, and it becometh unfruitful." Cares, riches, and the desire for things demand and receive the attention of one who merely professes to have given all to Christ. The Word is choked by divided allegiance. Many such people are never able to come to grips with these issues, so they continue to be fence-straddlers and never fulfill God's will for their lives.

The Bible tells of a young man who allowed something to come between him and Christ. He wanted the benefits of both worlds. He desired eternal life and asked Jesus how he could have it. He informed Jesus he had kept all the commandments since his youth. Apparently, he had not taken into account the commandment, "Thou shalt have no other gods before me," for Jesus read the secrets of his heart and said his riches would keep him from inheriting eternal life. This does not apply to all who are rich but to those whose riches come before God. For example, riches were not a problem for Barnabas and Zacchaeus. Jesus instructed him to disburse his riches to the poor. Unwilling to do so, the young man sadly went away, a terrible picture of one who endeavored to serve two masters. Worldly prosperity and the prestige that accompanies it were too appealing to his carnal mind. He could not give up these attractions. He is a sad reminder of today's country-club Christian.

Another scriptural example of those who wanted it both ways is found in Acts 5. Prior to this chapter, the early Christians had decided to pool their resources and share all their possessions. "They had all things common" (Acts 4:32). They sold their land and houses and brought the money they received from the sale to the apostles. "Distribution was made unto every man according as he had need" (Acts 4:35).

This was a noble, benevolent gesture made by the early church. Apparently, they made this decision of their own choosing because the Bible does not say God commanded them to do so. Nevertheless, since this was done by the saints at Jerusalem, it seems to be one of the identifying characteristics of this compassionate and sacrificial group. Apparently, this was indication that an individual had completely cast his lot for the cause of Christ.

Two people considered it so important to be identified with the saints that they chose to lie about the money they brought to the apostles. Ananias and his wife, Sapphira, brought part of the money from the sale of their land to the apostles under false pretense. They wanted to receive credit for something they hadn't done. They were under no requirement, no divine command, to bring the entire amount, but they lied about the money, saying it was the total price of the land. They set an example of deceitful conspiracy. They wanted to be recognized as part of this community-minded endeavor with those who had sacrificially made a benevolent commitment but selfishly kept part of the money for their own purposes.

Their divided allegiance can be seen today in those who waver on the threshold between two masters. Many want to exercise their independence and yet be associated with the righteous. Just as Ananias and Sapphira could not deceive God, neither can we have it both ways. We cannot expect to dance with the devil throughout the week and change partners and, in the assembly of the saints, deceive a few people. By doing so, we deceive no one more than we deceive ourselves.

The Word of God addresses those who are in danger of allowing the thorns to choke the Word in their lives. Jesus said, "Take heed to yourselves, lest at any time your hearts be overcharged with surfeiting, and drunkenness, and cares of this life and so that day come upon you unawares" (Luke 21:34). As believers, we need to take personal inventory to be sure we are not caught up with or overindulging in anything contrary to God.

> Love not the world, neither the things that are in the world. If any man loves the world, the love

> of the Father is not in him. For all that is in the world, the lust of the flesh, and the lust of the eyes, and the pride of life, is not of the Father but is of the world. And the world passeth away and the lust thereof: but he that doeth the will of God abideth forever.
>
> —1 John 2:15–17

The world has nothing good to offer, nor will it ever have anything good to offer, because it is contrary to God who is good, and it is influenced by Satan who is evil. Although Satan subtly paints a beautiful picture, his ultimate motive is "to steal, and to kill, and to destroy" (John 10:10). The world does not and cannot love the Church, and the Church must not love the world. Jesus said, "The world hateth you" (John 15:19). Believers should remember this each time the world casts an appealing shadow, each time they are inclined to please the world or to identify with it.

In Second Timothy is the account of a man who allowed his love for the world to cause him to forsake the way of righteousness. With death only a short time away, Paul wrote about it without fear (2 Timothy 4:6–8). His words were those of an overcomer, a conqueror, a victor, a finisher. Then, almost in the same instance, through the eyes of our imagination, we can see this courageous, stalwart aged apostle lay down his pen and break down and cry before writing the next two verses. He asked Timothy to come to him. Verse 10 explains the reason for his request, undoubtedly, the saddest words Paul ever wrote: "For Demas hath forsaken me, having loved this present world." Demas, who according to Philemon 24 had been a fellow laborer with Paul and also with men like Luke and Mark, had yielded to the allure of the world. What a waste! Yet this is the ultimate end of all who trifle with the world.

One of the prophecies concerning the plight of humankind in the last days declares that they will be "lovers of pleasure more than lovers of God" (2 Timothy 3:4). "Pleasure" is not wrong unless it diverts our attention from God who deserves our affection most. The world system, however, diligently promotes a flashy and magnetic appeal to pleasure and is successful far too many times. True Christians must have the courage to denounce any pleasure that competes with our love for God.

A pastor told of a young lady who became a Christian and served God faithfully for a time. At first, she was most sincere in her relationship with God. She was so devout she sought her pastor's counsel on almost every matter. Then her husband purchased a boat. She began to miss worship services, excusing her absence as the only day she and her husband could enjoy the boat together. Soon she was out of church completely. Her love for pleasure competed with her love for God. Unfortunately, love for pleasure won.

Another scripture warns against diversified duty: "No man that warreth entangleth himself with the affairs of this life" (2 Timothy 2:4). This does not mean a Christian cannot be a prosperous businessman, hold public office, be in civic clubs, or take part in community functions. However, he must be careful not to spread himself too thin. When the "busyness" of life reaches the point of entanglement and begins to take up time that rightfully belongs to God, the characteristics of the thorny-ground hearer can be seen: "The cares of this world and the lust of other things entering in, choke the word, and it becometh unfruitful" (Mark 4:19). When our busyness becomes of such magnitude, we do not have time for proper communion with God, we have too much to do. We can no longer "please him who hath chosen him to be a soldier" (2 Timothy 2:4).

The longer a person keeps one leg on the world's side of the fence, through the cares of life, covetousness, riches, pleasures, pride, or other entanglements, the easier it gets to be a friend of the world. James says this "spiritual adultery" places us in opposition to God: "Ye adulterers and adulteresses, know ye not that the friendship of the world is enmity with God? Whosoever therefore will be a friend of the world is the enemy of God" (James 4:4). He did not say being a friend of sinners, people in the world, was wrong; but being a friend of a system controlled by Satan, who is the adversary of God and believers, is wrong. Remember, more sinners come to a saving knowledge of Christ through Christians befriending them than any other way.

Be Not Conformed

Flirting with the world is risky business. In almost every such instance, a person is overcome by the world after, by the grace of God, he has been saved from it. Peter described this as an undesirable condition:

> For if after they have escaped the pollutions of the world through the knowledge of the Lord and Savior Jesus Christ, they are again entangled therein and overcome, the latter end is worse with them than the beginning. For it had been better for them not to have known the way of righteousness than, after they have known it, to turn from the holy commandment delivered unto them.
>
> —2 Peter 2:20–21

A mongrel society in the Old Testament set a double standard of half-heartedness and double-mindedness. "They feared the Lord and served their own gods" (2 Kings 17:33). This description could be applied to the country-club Christian who is trying to have the "best of both worlds." However, when a person loves the world so much that he becomes a friend of the world and is conformed to the world, he then is *of* the world—he is corrupted by the world and, finally, is overcome by the world. True Christians are not to be overcome by the world. Rather, we are to overcome the world (1 John 5:4).

Mature Christians must be aware of the world's problems and needs and also aware that the Church has help to offer—the good news of Jesus Christ. The Church must have compassion for the world's lost and be actively involved in witnessing to them. However, a believer must "keep himself unspotted from the world" (James 1:27). Above all, he must be sure that when the Lord returns, he is not straddling the fence that separates the Church and the world.

CHAPTER 4

Consecrated Christians

Various types of professing Christians have been discussed in the preceding chapters. In each case, however, the Word of God raises some questions about their relationship with Christ even though they are called Christians.

In every generation, there have been weak Christians, borderline Christians, and hypocrites. But in every generation, there have also been those who have patterned their lives after good character examples and according to the infallible instructions recorded in God's holy Word.

Even in the time of Malachi with its apathy, profaneness, and rebellion, there was still a people who "feared the Lord" (Malachi 3:16). In John 6, Jesus gave a great discourse on the Bread of Life, and during that one sermon over five thousand people walked out on Him. At a time when such a vast number chose not to accept the truth, twelve realized there was no alternate route to eternal life.

Throughout history, some have remained faithful to God no matter the circumstances or requirements. The Word of God says, "His truth endureth to all generations" (Psalms 100:5). Even in the twenty-first century, with apostasy all around, there are still those who have determined in their hearts to serve God and apply the truths of His Word to their lives daily. No title can be more fitting to describe them than "consecrated Christians."

Dedication

A consecrated Christian is dedicated to the service and worship of God. He gives his all, making a total commitment to the Lord. This world holds no attraction for the consecrated Christian. His only interest in it is to fulfill the purpose for which God has placed him here. He realizes this world is temporal, and any mark he makes here will be of no eternal significance except as he impacts someone with the love of God and the message of Calvary.

The consecrated Christian doesn't worry, fear, or panic when he sees troublesome and perilous times. He continues his simple walk of faith that assumes the attitude of the wise writer who said, "Trust in the Lord with all thine heart; and lean not unto thine own understanding. In all thy ways, acknowledge him, and he shall direct thy paths" (Proverbs 3:5–6). During a period of heavy trials, the wise and patient Job said, "The righteous also shall hold on his way, and he that hath clean hands shall be stronger and stronger" (Job 17:9). This powerful statement of faith is also indicative of the thinking of the believer who has given all in God's service.

The word *consecrate* in Scripture is the English translation of various Hebrew and Greek words which mean "separate, to be set apart, devote, to fill the hands." *Webster* adds another definition: "to cause to be revered; hallow." All these definitions can be seen in the character of a person who is totally resolved to follow Christ. King David posed a question that should challenge every concerned believer: "Who then is willing to consecrate his service this day unto the Lord?" (1 Chronicles 29:5). A brief look at each meaning of the word *consecrate* will help clarify what it means to be a consecrated Christian.

Separation

The consecrated Christian is one who is separate from the world and the unclean. The Church has been "called out" by God and separated. Jesus said, "Ye are not of the world, but I have chosen you out of the world" (John 15:19). The scriptural admonition is to "come out from among them, and be ye separate, saith the Lord, and touch not the unclean thing" (2 Corinthians 6:17).

In the Old Testament, the strictest vow an individual could make concerned separation. A Nazarite, recorded in Numbers 6:1–18, vowed to not defile himself by touching anything unclean. In another example, Abraham was told to get out of his country and away from his kindred and his father's house (see Genesis 12:1). His homeland was a place of idol worship. Consecration is separation from uncleanness in any form.

In answer to David's question, the consecrated Christian boldly responds according to Scripture: "Let us cleanse ourselves from all filthiness of the flesh and spirit" (2 Corinthians 7:1). Such blessed saints can still be seen in the Church, clinging to what is sacred and separated from that which would defile.

The consecrated Christian realizes he has been set apart for service in God's kingdom. Just as the vessels of the Old Testament tabernacle were set apart for the service of the Lord, so each New Testament believer is a vessel which should be set apart for God's service. In Exodus 30:30, Aaron and his sons were set apart to minister unto the Lord as priests. Believers today are also to be set apart to minister unto the Lord. Scripture says Christians are a "royal priesthood that ye should shew forth the praises of him who hath called you out of darkness into his marvelous light" (1 Peter 2:9). The consecrated Christian will be found ministering to the Lord. He will answer David's question by presenting himself before the Lord "a vessel unto honor, sanctified, and meet for the master's use, and prepared unto every good work" (2 Timothy 2:21). He knows "the Lord hath set apart him that is godly for himself" (Psalms 4:3).

Devotion

The consecrated Christian is totally devoted to the Lord—spirit, soul, and body. He realizes he is not his own, but he is bought with a price. Such devotion causes believers to first present themselves to the Lord and then present their time, talent, and possessions to the Lord.

The churches of Macedonia are great examples of consecration. While they gave of their temporal means even beyond their power, they "first gave their own selves to the Lord" (2 Corinthians 8:1–5). The beauty of selflessness is obvious. Such a consecrated Christian displays a total emptying of self so that Christ is all in all. He answers David's question, "I will present my body a living sacrifice unto the Lord" (Romans 12:1).

The word *consecrate* in Scripture also means to have one's hands filled in service to the Lord. The word is used numerous times in the sense of "filling the hands." We cannot serve God with empty hands. Neither can we bless others with empty hands. The consecrated Christian does not allow his hands to become so full of other things that he cannot be of service to God. He seeks for God to fill his hands so he can distribute to others and satisfy hungry souls. He is found filled with the Word of God, the Spirit of God, and the love of God, and he shares this fullness with others.

Worship

Consecrated Christians prompt others to revere or hallow God. They praise God and uplift His name. They continually endeavor to bring honor to God and His kingdom. In answer to David's question, the consecrated Christian says, "I will bless the Lord at all times: his praise shall continually be in my mouth" (Psalms 34:1). These true worshipers, who worship God in spirit and in truth, can still be found today.

The consecrated Christian is a combination of all the definitions discussed. The characteristics are available to all who profess Christ—all point to those who have completely sold out to Christ. Such believers have given all, forsaken all, denied self, and have taken up their cross and are following Jesus. They "walk in the light as he is in the light" (1 John 1:7). They continue in His Word, proving they are His disciples indeed (John 8:31). They have put on the whole armor of God (Ephesians 6:11). They do not count their lives dear unto themselves (Acts 20:24).

A Lifestyle

Consecrated Christians are not shaken when storms rage. Their simple walk of faith causes them to say, "I reckon that the sufferings of this present time are not worthy to be compared with the glory which shall be revealed in us" (Romans 8:18). They realize they are only sojourning in this world. Therefore, they can boldly say,

> For which cause we faint not but though our outward man perish, yet the inward man is renewed day by day.
>
> For our light affliction, which is but for a moment, worketh for us a far more exceeding and eternal weight of glory; While we look not at the things which are seen but at the things which are not seen: for the things which are seen are temporal; but the things which are not seen are eternal.
>
> —2 Corinthians 4:16–18

They, like Christ, have endured the cross and will continue to do so until Christ calls them home (see Hebrews 12:2).

These determined believers are found in all age groups and in all places. They sacrifice meals. They sacrifice sleep. They sacrifice time, money, and self because of their love for God and humankind. Because of such devotion, the Church will be triumphant. When asked why they are willing to pay such a price, consecrated Christians, from a heart consecrated to God, respond, "He must increase, but I must decrease" (John 3:30).

Let all who are called Christians realize the need for such consecration to fulfill God's will in their lives. To be identified by the name of Christ carries with it the responsibility and obligation to live a life of consecration. May we stir up the gift of God within us! Let all who profess Christ also possess Christlikeness.

SECTION 2

The following chapters focus on the Antioch Church where the disciples were first called Christians. A study of the Christlike attributes of the saints in Antioch will help us understand why they were so appropriately named after that name above every name. The name has remained approximately two thousand years. The Church must live up to it!

CHAPTER 5

The Antioch Example: Teaching

The first four chapters dealt with various types of people who are called Christians. Upon reviewing the lifestyles of these professing believers, we can see some who are indeed Christlike as outlined in Scripture, but we can also see some who cause us to question how closely their lifestyle aligns with the Word of God. Clearly, not all who are called Christians are truly consecrated. We can rest assured, however, that those who were the first to be called Christians were indeed everything the name implies.

"And the disciples were called Christians first in Antioch" (Acts 11:26). Since the name was first given at Antioch, we should look to the origin of the name to better connect our profession with the example of the saints of Antioch. What a great honor bestowed upon the saints at Antioch to be called Christians! Not only was the name first given there, but it is also the only time it is used in Scripture in its plural form.

Some scholars believe the name was given as a nickname in mockery of those who professed faith in Christ. Others believe the name was given either by the citizens or civic authorities simply as a title of distinction. Still others believe the name was given by Euodius when he was a bishop of Antioch. Whatever the reason, whether given in honor or in mockery, the name remains appropriate today—appropriate because it was given to the followers of Christ, the Anointed One.

Equally important is what the name means: Christlikeness. The Christians were anointed by the same Spirit who anointed Christ.

This name was given because their lifestyle was evident before it was named. As the world looks on our life, they will name it. As believers, we should live in such a way that others would name us after Christ. We should publicize the name of Christ through our lifestyle. What better way for the world to get a clearer understanding of the title given to believers than to study the attributes of those to whom it was first given?

This chapter and those following will each discuss a Christlike characteristic of the church where the name "Christian" was first applied. These same qualities were also evident in the early church at Jerusalem from which came the men who began the church at Antioch and was itself begun by those who had been with Jesus. Additional New Testament examples will show how these Christlike qualities were handed down from Christ through the early church and should still be considered part of the heritage of believers if we are to indeed exemplify Christlikeness as the name "Christians" implies.

The Antioch Example

The disciples of Antioch saw the need for sound instruction in the Word of God even in the early development of their church. Three references strongly point to the fact teaching was an ongoing process in Antioch:

1. "And it came to pass, that a whole year they [Barnabas and Saul] assembled themselves with the church [at Antioch], and taught much people" (Acts 11:26).
2. "Now there were in the church that was at Antioch certain prophets and teachers" (Acts 13:1).
3. Paul and Barnabas "continued in Antioch, teaching and preaching the Word of the Lord, with many others also" (Acts 15:35).

From the early days of its existence, the Antioch Church displayed a teachable spirit and an eagerness to learn the truth. It was blessed with and characterized by solid teaching and good teachers.

Are local churches today characterized by sound instruction? God is saving and placing in the church today young converts who express a desire to learn the truth and who need to be instructed properly. These eager young converts must be soundly indoctrinated in the early days of their Christian existence.

Others, not yet converted, are seeking a church that will teach them truth. When these sincere potential converts see genuine, scriptural instruction occurring, they will be drawn to such an environment. Are our churches providing such an environment of learning? Some churches do not advocate teaching for fear it will cause less spiritual fervor. This fear is unfounded, and such a belief is erroneous. The teaching at Antioch certainly did not prevent spiritual fires from burning. Proper indoctrination will only make sincere hearts burn with greater intensity.

Christ—the Supreme Example

The abundance of teachers and the desire for teaching are good reasons the disciples at Antioch were called Christians. Their namesake, Christ, was the supreme example of greatness in teaching. He taught almost constantly in the gospels. He taught in the synagogues. He taught by the seashore. He taught from aboard Peter's ship.

Mark 6:31–34 is a touching narrative showing Jesus's concern that the people be soundly indoctrinated. He and the disciples had separated themselves from the people for a period of rest and leisure. When the crowds came to where Jesus was, He was "moved with compassion toward them because they were as sheep not having a shepherd: and he began to teach them many things" (verse 34). The great teacher saw people without a sense of direction, not knowing what to do, and gave them instruction. He still has compassion for His people and is pleased when He sees His example of teaching being followed.

In Matthew 5–7, Christ taught at length in the Sermon on the Mount practical applications for a life of happiness, contentment, and godliness. Beginning with the beatitudes in chapter 5, the great teacher related the requirements for being blessed and the rewards.

In chapter 6, He shared four key ingredients to a life of contentment: giving, forgiveness, prayer, and fasting. In chapter 7, He forbade judgmental and self-righteous attitudes and taught the golden rule. He also talked about two ways in life: the broad and the narrow. He ended this great discourse by declaring all who adhere to His teaching are wise, but those who do not are foolish.

After Christ's longest recorded discourse, the people responded, "He taught them as one having authority" (Matthew 7:29). The Sermon on the Mount was at the beginning of His ministry where He set the supreme example of the need for teaching. The young church at Antioch was quick to follow His example. Those who are called Christians today must do the same.

John 6 relates Christ's discourse on the Bread of Life. Although many felt His instructions were too hard, Peter realized He had spoken "the words of eternal life" (verse 68). Christ knew how important it was that the people be taught. Luke 24 tells of the saddened Emmaus Road disciples on the day of Jesus's resurrection. Jesus, realizing their need for proper understanding, compassionately took time to teach them. Verse 27 records, "He expounded unto them, in all the scriptures, the things concerning himself." Verse 32 says their hearts burned as He opened the Scriptures.

Hearts still burn when Christ's example is followed, and the Word of God is taught. Nicodemus perhaps said it best in John 3:2 when he called Jesus "a teacher come from God." He was a teacher sent from heaven with a heavenly message that will take people to heaven as it continues to be taught and obeyed.

Before ascending to heaven, His instructions in the Great Commission were to "go teach all nations, teaching them to observe all things whatsoever I have commanded you" (Matthew 28:19–20).

Is the Christlike attribute of teaching prevalent in contemporary churches? Or are some churches more caught up in selfishly fulfilling their own desires and dreams rather than obeying Christ who said, "Teach all nations" and "Learn of me" (Matthew 11:29)?

Perhaps every church should ask: "If our church existed in the time of the Antioch Church, would we be enough like Christ to be called Christians by those who observed our lives?"

The Early Church Example

The saints at Antioch had not been with Christ. Therefore, the saints of the early church at Jerusalem were the connecting link in the chain between Christ and Antioch. Men from Jerusalem began the work at Antioch. The church at Jerusalem was begun by men called apostles who had been with Christ. These men possessed Christlike attributes and continued His message. They set the Christlike example for those who carried it to Antioch.

With regard to teaching, the early church is said to have "continued steadfastly in the apostles' doctrine" (Acts 2:42). "Daily, they ceased not to teach and preach Jesus Christ" (Acts 5:42). Having been with the greatest teacher, they realized the importance of being taught and of teaching others.

When the church at Jerusalem heard about the new work at Antioch, they sent Barnabas, an experienced teacher and preacher of the Word, to ensure this church was properly indoctrinated from its embryonic stages. Many churches, that have existed for many years, still suffer because sound doctrine was not laid down at their foundation. But Barnabas, "a good man, and full of the Holy Ghost and faith" (Acts 11:24), was so concerned that this church gets good instruction from its beginning that he sought the assistance of Saul. "Then departed Barnabas to Tarsus, for to seek Saul: And when he had found him, he brought him unto Antioch. And it came to pass, that a whole year, they assembled themselves with the church and taught much people" (Acts 11:25–26).

While visiting sinners and inviting them to church, a pastor encountered a young man who was unsaved. The young man had been exposed to church quite a bit and had seen both genuine and phony occurrences in church services. Such experiences had left him somewhat disillusioned. His desire was to find a church that would lead him to Christ and teach him to live a Christlike lifestyle, using the Word of God as a foundation. Good teaching is still essential.

Additional New Testament Examples

The early church continued to hand down this wonderful ministry of teaching, which is an important part of the heritage of the church. Paul, one of the early teachers at Antioch, "continued there (at Corinth) a year and six months, teaching the Word of God among them" (Acts 18:11). This was six months longer than he spent in his first teaching assignment in Antioch, for he realized how essential instruction is to the church. In his first letter to the church at Corinth, he placed special emphasis on teaching: "And God hath set some in the church, first apostles, secondarily prophets, thirdly teachers, after that miracles, then gifts of healings, helps, governments, diversities of tongues" (1 Corinthians 12:28). We can assume that Paul, through the inspiration of the Holy Spirit, placed these blessings from God in order of priority since he used such words as *first*, *secondarily*, *thirdly*, *after that*, and *then*.

Notice the importance he gave to teachers by placing them *before* miracles, gifts of healing, and diversities of tongues. While all are important and have been set in the Church by God to complement one another, such gifts as miracles, healings, and tongues need to be regulated by sound, scriptural doctrine to protect against mimicry, misuse, and abuse. No doubt that is why Paul said, "Thirdly teachers, after that miracles, then healings, tongues." The church at Corinth needed this teaching because their use of the gifts had gotten out of hand. Paul instructed them in chapters 12–14 on the proper governing of the gifts so the use of the gifts would both edify the Church and bring glory to God. Perhaps some churches today need to rearrange their priorities in accordance with 1 Corinthians 12:28.

Closely related to teaching is having a teachable spirit. Those who think they have acquired so much knowledge that there is nothing more to learn have an unteachable or exalted spirit. Such people are usually argumentative and have a question for every answer. Any individual, any local congregation, or any denomination that allows this to happen has, in essence, said teaching is no longer necessary and has laid aside this Christlike quality. The Word of God says such a person should "take heed lest he fall" (1 Corinthians 10:12).

> The following illustration, titled "The Living Thief," is a good example of one who is unteachable: A minister of the gospel was trying to impress upon a certain man his obligation to live a consistent Christian life. He sought to convince him of his responsibility to be obedient to the Word of God. When asked if he had ever been baptized, the man replied, "No sir, I haven't, but why should I? The dying thief was never baptized, and he went to heaven." When the preacher urged him to be more faithful in church attendance, the other answered, "Why should I? The dying thief didn't go to church, and he was saved." Finally, the man's pastor spoke to him about the matter of giving and his duty to support the work of the local assembly with his financial giving. To that the man responded, "That's not necessary. The dying thief went to heaven, and he never gave one cent to missions or anything like that." Turning away, the man of God said with disgust in his voice, "Mister, the only difference I can see between you and the thief on the cross is this, 'He was a dying thief, and you are a living one.'"

Scripture records an example of a good teacher who also had a teachable spirit. Apollos was "an eloquent man," "mighty in the scriptures," and "fervent in the spirit," who spoke "boldly in the synagogue" (see Acts 18:24–28). These verses also say he "was instructed in the way of the Lord" and "spake and taught diligently the things of the Lord." Obviously, he was instructed *and* he taught others. Aquila and Priscilla observed him and realized he needed to be more thoroughly indoctrinated. "They took him unto them and expounded unto him the way of God more perfectly" (verse 26).

Our knowledge of God's Word will never be so great we cannot learn more. The teachable spirit of Apollos will always be a valuable asset to the Church. How else can believers teach others unless they first have a desire to be taught? Because of his teachable spirit, Apollos watered where Paul had planted (1 Corinthians 3:6). Paul was a great teacher. Following him could only be done by someone who knew the importance of continual instruction. Are we not also called to follow Paul and a host of other teachers in carrying on the Christlike example of teaching? Did not Christ command it in the Great Commission? Is it not imperative that the body of Christ do so today?

In Ephesians 4:11, Paul identified the ministry gifts Christ gave to the church: "And he gave some, apostles; and some, prophets; and some, evangelists; and some, pastors and teachers." He proceeded to clarify the purpose of the ministry gifts: "For the perfecting of the saints, for the work of the ministry, for the edifying of the body of Christ" (Ephesians 4:12). To accomplish this purpose, all the gifts identified must function. Paul also said a man who was to hold the office of bishop had to be "apt to teach" (1 Timothy 3:2). This simply meant he had to be "skilled in teaching" to oversee the flock of God.

Few today seem as attracted to the teaching ministry as they are to other ministries, although teaching is vitally important. But Paul, one of the most effective teachers of the Word of God, continued in his epistles to show the necessity of the God-sent gift of teaching to the Church. Even the last verse of this book of power—the outpouring of the Holy Spirit, the beginning of the Church and its phenomenal growth, miracles, healings, manifestations of the Holy Ghost—addressed this ministry with Paul "teaching those things which concern the Lord Jesus Christ with all confidence, no man forbidding him" (Acts 28:31).

Teaching through the Ages

The importance of teaching is evident throughout the New Testament. Christ came to earth as the supreme example of a teacher. The apostles began the early church at Jerusalem with the doctrines of Christ. That teaching has been handed down through the centuries and still exists. God never intended for teaching to take a back seat in the church. The Antioch Church realized this even in its formative stages. They practiced what Christ, the great teacher, had done. No wonder they were called Christians. Those today who are called Christians should diligently endeavor to maintain this edifying attribute of Christ.

CHAPTER 6

The Antioch Example: Worship

We can give no nobler performance than to worship our Creator. Worship is our greatest act. Worship is our chief function. We have no higher purpose in life. The psalmist was divinely inspired when he said, "O come, let us worship and bow down: let us kneel before the Lord our maker" (Psalm 95:6). In Psalm 107:8, 15, 21, 31 he redundantly pleaded, "Oh that men would praise the Lord for his goodness and for his wonderful works to the children of men!" Worship is the way the creature acknowledges the "worthship" of the Creator. As believers worship, we minister to the Lord.

The many words translated "worship" in the Bible fall into two categories. The first category deals with an attitude of adoration and submission and the idea of bowing down. The second involves acts of labor, work, sacrifice, and service. Both are ways of acknowledging that the Creator is deserving of such ministry. Therefore, as long as believers display an attitude of adoration for God or perform an act of service for God in spirit and in truth, we are true worshipers. The heavenly Father desires such worship. All who are called Christians should desire to please the heavenly Father. Those at Antioch were a worshiping congregation and, like their namesake Christ, wanted to please their Father in heaven.

The Antioch Example

The Christlike attribute of teaching discussed in chapter 5 was surely effective at Antioch. Good instruction at the foundation of this outstanding young church had helped to develop other fine qualities, including worship. Those teachers at Antioch "ministered to the Lord, and fasted" (Acts 13:2). In this statement, both categories of worship can be seen: the attitude of adoration and the act of sacrifice. The Antioch believers worshiped diligently, even to the extent of self-denial. And as they worshiped, they received instruction from God.

After they heard from God, they took time to worship again before taking action: "And when they had fasted and prayed and laid their hands on them, they sent them away" (verse 3). What a beautiful scene of worship and its effects! They ministered to the Lord and fasted. God spoke, and they fasted, prayed, and obeyed. Perhaps when we, as believers, do not hear from God, we lack an attitude of adoration, of submission, of bowing down. Perhaps we also lack in acts of labor, service, and sacrifice when we do not hear God speak words of instruction.

The Christians at Antioch directed all worship to God to whom it rightfully belongs. In both adoration and acts of service, their motive was to love God and bring glory to Him, which should be the motive of all worship. This was not the case of one man who stood during a testimony service in his church to "worship" God. He told of his love for God and all he had done for God. He mentioned his witnessing, his Bible reading, and his praying. He told of praying for long periods in a little workshop behind his house. He even told of how he had worn out his pants at the knees. He verbally expressed his love for his fellowman. When he finally sat down, God had not received much adoration and glory. Instead, "worship" had been directed toward the man.

Another account of misdirected worship involved a young pastor who was curious about those church services from bygone days—the '30s, '40s, and '50s—he had heard about that commonly continued past midnight. Although the services sounded wonderful, he had always been puzzled as to what actually transpired in the services. The son of a godly and closed-mouth mother, he could not get any information from her. She was one of those rare people who, if she could not say something good, would not say anything. This puzzled the young pastor even more, for he didn't believe she would withhold anything from him that would be edifying.

One day another relative shared some insightful comments about some of those past-midnight service dismissals. During the last two to four hours of the service, the same people would take turns, usually for about thirty minutes each, walking back and forth across the floor, supposedly giving a praise report for God. Ultimately, they advised people how to live and, in essence, competed with one another in delivering their so-called testimonies. They spent quantity time but not quality time worshiping.

What would happen now if a church spent three or four hours in true worship, either corporate or private, and in acts of service and adoration to God?

Christ—the Supreme Example

Just as Christ was the supreme example of a teacher, He was also the greatest example of a worshiper. In John 4:23–24, He told the woman of Samaria that the heavenly Father was seeking true worshipers, those who would worship Him in spirit and in truth. His earthly life is a portrait of one with an attitude of submission, adoration, and bowing down to His Father in worship. The gospels also portray Him as one who constantly performed acts of service to humankind and thereby worshiped His Father through labor and sacrifice. Acts 10:38 says He "went about doing good and healing all that were oppressed of the devil; for God was with him."

A study of Christ's private worship is spiritually inspiring. He rose early in the morning to commune with His Heavenly Father.

> And in the morning, rising up a great while before day, he went out and departed into a solitary place and there prayed.
>
> —Mark 1:35

He felt the need to begin His day with His Father. Christ believed "men ought always to pray" (Luke 18:1).

According to Mark 6:46, "And when he had sent them [the people] away, he departed into a mountain to pray." Verses 47 and 48 indicate that He began praying in the evening and did not come to the disciples until early morning, suggesting He spent the night alone with God. In fact, He often prayed the entire night. Luke 6:12 says, "He went out into a mountain to pray and continued all night in prayer to God." Interestingly, the day following His all-night prayer, He chose His twelve disciples. Christ here set an example of talking to the heavenly Father before making a decision or taking action. Shouldn't His followers do the same? The disciples at Antioch certainly did!

A valuable lesson can be learned from the timing of this prayer, which began immediately after the miraculous feeding of the five thousand. Do we take time to worship after God has solved our problems or met our need? As a rule, more time is spent asking God to meet the need than thanking Him once the need is met. Christ, however, prayed long hours after the miracle had taken place.

Mark 6:47–52 tells of another need that arose in the early morning hours. Christ, who had been communing with His Father, walked upon the stormy sea and rescued His disciples from the storm. If believers will follow His pattern of praying often, both before and after the problem, we will be better able to walk through life's storms.

At times, Jesus chose solitude to gain strength through prayer. In Luke 5:15–16, the multitudes gathered around Him to have their needs met. His response? "He withdrew himself into the wilderness, and prayed" (verse 16). If Christ needed solitary communion with the Father, then certainly His followers need to follow His example.

Jesus often prayed when His disciples were with Him (Luke 9:18, 11:1). Apparently, the disciples noticed His disciplined prayer life and, realizing how important worship was to His ministry of power, asked Him to teach them to pray (Luke 11:1). He responded by giving them what has traditionally been called "The Lord's Prayer." This model prayer addresses the Father and acknowledges the "worthship" of the Father. It is still an excellent pattern for the believer to follow when worshiping.

Jesus not only worshiped by spending much time in secret prayer, but He also worshiped publicly. Each time the feeding of the hungry multitude is recorded, Jesus gave thanks prior to distributing the food. In Matthew 11:25, He publicly prayed, "I thank thee, O Father, Lord of heaven and earth, because thou has hid these things from the wise and prudent and hast revealed them unto babes."

Before raising Lazarus from the dead, Jesus looked up and said, "Father, I thank thee that thou hast heard me. And I knew that thou hearest me always: but because of the people which stand by I said it, that they may believe that thou hast sent me" (John 11:41–42). On the last night of His earthly life, before going to the garden for private prayer, Jesus prayed the priestly prayer of intercession to the Father in John 17.

Jesus also set the example in public worship through His attendance in the sanctuary.

> As His custom was, he went into the synagogue on the sabbath day.
>
> —Luke 4:16

Hebrews 10:25 admonishes believers to continue coming together in corporate worship. Can those who profess to follow Him be truly Christlike if we do not do as He did? Referring to His Father in John 8:29, Jesus said, "For I do always those things that please him." The desire of every Christian should be for worship to be of such consistent quality that it will please the heavenly Father.

There was no lack of worship in the life of Christ. In His last few hours, He was in the garden of Gethsemane communing with His Father and submitting His will to His Father's will. Even in His dying moments, while hanging on the Cross, He continued talking to the Father. Every believer should determine to do likewise until our time comes to depart this earthly life. We should be found ministering to the Lord like those at Antioch where they were first called Christians.

The Early Church Example

The characteristic of worship at the Antioch Church, like that of teaching, was handed down from the early church at Jerusalem. By being with Christ and observing Him, the apostles knew how imperative worship was, so it became a practice of the early church from its beginning. Before Pentecost they "were continually in the temple, praising and blessing God" (Luke 24:53). Acts 1:14 says, "These all continued with one accord in prayer and supplication." According to Acts 2:1, this worship continued until Pentecost: "And when the day of Pentecost was fully come, they were all with one accord in one place." This is how the church began—in worship. Such a Christlike quality must be carried on.

The saints at Jerusalem did not relax their efforts in worship after Pentecost. Some Christians have a tendency to coast after a phenomenal outpouring of blessing from God, but not the early church. They continued daily, with one accord, to praise God (Acts 2:46–47). Can we do less and still please God?

Many today will not worship unless things are going smoothly and there are not problems, but this was not true of the early church. They continued to worship even with the threat of persecution. After the healing of the lame man in Acts 3, Peter and John were arrested. Their captors, not knowing what to do with them, threatened them and told them not to speak or teach anymore in the name of Jesus (Acts 4:18). Upon their release, Peter and John went to their fellow Christians and told them of the warning they had received. The early church, however, did not fret or worry; instead, they began to worship. Acts 4:24–31 details their worship and its results: "And when they heard that [the warning of the opposition], they lifted up their voice to God with one accord and said, Lord, thou art God" (verse 24). Unpleasant circumstances did not make God any less worthy of adoration. Worship was a lifestyle of the early church and was carried on by those who went out from Jerusalem to begin new churches.

When discussing worship in the early church, we should observe the church leaders at Jerusalem, for a church is no stronger than its leaders. Acts 6 records a situation concerning worship that involved the apostles. The Grecians were murmuring because their widows were being neglected in the distribution of food. The apostles responded by saying they should not lay aside the Word of God to handle such matters. But as wise, organized, Spirit-filled, and Spirit-directed men, they delegated this responsibility to others. As Church leaders, they believed worship was most important and should take priority in their lives. In fact, the apostles said, "We will give ourselves continually to prayer and to the ministry of the word" (Acts 6:4).

Undoubtedly, the Jerusalem Church was characterized by such worship because of the priority placed on worship by the early church leaders. The apostles had followed the supreme example of Christ. They then inspired and taught others to worship, who in turn carried the practice to Antioch where they ministered to the Lord.

Additional New Testament Examples

The New Testament includes many examples of worship. The early church continued to follow Christ's lifestyle of worship and continued to hand it down to others, making it still a part of the heritage of the Church.

Acts 16 records an outstanding New Testament worship scene involving Paul and Silas. The two had been arrested, beaten, imprisoned, and placed in stocks for the sake of the gospel. What might others have done in this situation? Some might have renounced Christ. No doubt, some would have begged for mercy. However, those willing to die for the cause of Christ would likely do so with dignity. For example, they might say to each other, "Let's not cry or beg. If they release us, fine; if they kill us, fine. Let's go to our execution with a smile. Let's be glad to be martyrs for Christ. Let's die with dignity."

This, however, was not the case with Paul and Silas. They probably had been humiliated and taunted both by their captors and the other inmates. "Where is your God now? What are you going to do with your God now?" We can imagine those preachers answering, "We're going to worship Him." The hecklers, taken aback by such a reply, then said, "You mean you feel like worshiping your God in your condition?" The men of God probably responded truthfully and determinedly, "No, we don't feel like it, but we're going to worship God anyhow."

Worship is not contingent upon our feelings. With their backs lacerated and bleeding and their feet fast in stocks, Paul and Silas worshiped their heavenly Father.

> At midnight, Paul and Silas prayed and sang praises unto God.
>
> —Acts 16:25

Some of God's greatest blessings await those who press through all obstacles to worship Him. In the case of Paul and Silas, they were liberated and led the jailer and his household to the Lord. May the church today be a worshiping church that leads others to the Lord!

Paul encouraged the worship lifestyle in his epistles. In Romans 12:1, he appealed "that ye present your bodies a living sacrifice, holy, acceptable unto God, *which is your reasonable service*." Other translations help to clarify that last phrase. The *Revised Standard Version* says, "Which is your spiritual worship." The *New Testament in Basic English* states, "Which is the worship, it is right for you to give him." The *Knox Translation* says, "This is the worship due from you as rational creatures." Paul stressed the right and rational thing to do is to offer our very selves to God in worship.

The chief apostle also said worship is to be constant. In 1 Thessalonians 5:16–17, he admonished, "Rejoice evermore. Pray without ceasing." In Philippians 4:4, he exhorted, "Rejoice in the Lord always: and again I say, Rejoice." We can worship Him willingly now or later without choice. According to Paul, someday everyone will acknowledge He is Lord. "That at the name of Jesus, every knee should bow of things in heaven and things in earth and things under the earth; and that every tongue should confess that Jesus Christ is Lord to the glory of God the Father" (Philippians 2:10–11). We should worship willingly.

Another New Testament worship scene takes us into heaven. John, who had been taken there in the Spirit, shared what he witnessed in heaven in Revelation 4 and 5. Four creatures worshiped around the throne continually.

> They rest not day and night, saying, Holy, holy, holy, Lord God Almighty, which was, and is, and is to come.
>
> —Revelation 4:8

As the four creatures worshiped, twenty-four elders, whose seats were around the throne, fell down before the lord and cast their crowns before the throne, saying,

> Thou art worthy, O Lord, to receive glory and honor and power: for thou has created all things, and for thy pleasure they are and were created.
>
> —Revelation 4:11

This beautiful scene escalates into a crescendo of praise when the four creatures, and twenty-four elders were joined by a large company of angels.

> The number of them was ten thousand times ten thousand and thousands of thousands; Saying with a loud voice, Worthy is the Lamb that was slain to receive power, and riches, and wisdom, and strength, and honor, and glory, and blessing.
>
> —Revelation 5:11–12

What wonderful worship! Worship is the chief occupation of these heavenly creatures. Shouldn't it be the pursuit of the Church on earth?

Worship Through the Ages

Christ, the namesake of Christians and the builder and head of the Church, is the supreme example of one who worshiped His

Heavenly Father. The early church followed His example in worship and handed it down to future believers. God desires worship. He inhabits, or resides, in the praises of His people. The Antioch Church, where the disciples were first called Christians, ministered to the Lord. They were worshipers. Like Jesus, they desired to please their heavenly Father. They reminded others of Christ.

When worship ceases to be of paramount importance to professing believers, it is then that we cease to possess an important Christlike attribute. This cannot happen to the true Church!

CHAPTER 7

The Antioch Example: Direction by the Holy Spirit

> If we live in the Spirit, let us also walk in the Spirit.
>
> —Galatians 5:25

Paul wrote this wise instruction after telling of the warfare of the flesh and the Spirit and after exposing both the works of the flesh and the fruit of the Spirit. He introduced this subject by saying, "Walk in the Spirit, and ye shall not fulfill the lust of the flesh" (Galatians 5:16). Twice, both at the beginning and at the end of this passage, the Word says, "Walk in the Spirit."

Life in the Spirit begins when a person is born again. This being the case, Paul says we should walk in the Spirit also. To walk in the Spirit means to be led, guided, or directed by the Spirit. Therefore, all who are called Christians are to be directed by the Holy Spirit in our actions. He must guide our walk, our talk, and our lifestyle.

Through human knowledge alone, we do not know how to perform life's duties in a way that will please God. God advises His children who are trying futilely to figure out what to do in a troublesome situation, "Not by might, nor by power, but by my spirit, saith the Lord of hosts" (Zechariah 4:6). No amount of physical ability or political ingenuity will solve the problems we face. This can only be done through the work and direction of God's Holy Spirit.

To the seven churches in Revelation 2 and 3, Christ repeated the same advice: "He that hath an ear, let him hear what the Spirit saith unto the churches." What the Spirit says to each believer and to the Church is of utmost importance. To walk outside the direction of the Holy Spirit is to be outside God's will. To be outside God's will ought to be the most disturbing thing in the lives of those who are called Christians. To desire to be in the Father's will is to be like Christ who said, "I do always those things that please him" (John 8:29).

The direction of the Holy Spirit will lead believers to *where* God wants us to be, *when* God wants us to be there, doing *what* God wants us to do, and doing it the *way* God wants it to be done. This is the essence of God's will. The desire for such direction can be clearly seen in the congregation at Antioch.

The Antioch Example

The Antioch Church is an ideal example of those who believed in and sought for the direction of the Holy Spirit. The first recorded example was in the early days of the church, apparently in its second year. Immediately after the name "Christians" was first applied to the believers at Antioch, the inspired writer proceeded to tell of a prophet named Agabus who came to Antioch from the church at Jerusalem (Acts 11:27–28). Under the influence of the Holy Spirit, he foretold of a famine that was to come. The reaction of the disciples at Antioch showed their reverence for and belief in what the Spirit said to the church. They decided to help the poor saints in Jerusalem through the famine when it came as the Spirit said it would. This Christlike act of benevolence is discussed further in chapter 8.

Another example of the Antioch Church being Spirit-directed is found in Acts 13:2, the same portion of scripture referred to in the previous chapters about the teachers and worshipers at Antioch. The verse deals with the commissioning of specific individuals: "As they ministered to the Lord, and fasted, the Holy Ghost said, "Separate me Barnabas and Saul for the work whereunto I have called them." This divine call is of major importance because it signified the beginning of a new missionary outreach. The Holy Spirit was specific in naming the individuals, but the specific details of their mission are not revealed.

The Spirit does not always give all the details of a matter at once, but He will always reveal what needs to be known in time for it to be effective. The important thing here is the reverent obedience of the Christians of Antioch. They heard what the Spirit said: "And when they had fasted and prayed and laid their hands on them, they sent them away" (Acts 13:3). The Spirit's command had been to set apart, or dedicate, Barnabas and Saul for God's service. This they did, and verse 4 says they were "sent forth by the Holy Ghost."

At Antioch, the Holy Ghost was the chief administrator. To receive favor from the heavenly Father, He must also be the leader in every church and in the personal lives of all who are called Christians. May God help all believers both to see and follow the example set by this amazing young church at Antioch. How well they epitomize those who are called Christians! How well they exemplify their namesake Christ!

Christ—the Supreme Example

A study of the earthly ministry of Christ shows He was led by the Spirit. However, we do not have to make a complete study of His life to ascertain this. When Jesus was baptized, the Holy Ghost descended upon Him (Luke 3:22). Luke 4:1 says, "And Jesus, being full of the Holy Ghost, returned from Jordan and was led by the Spirit into the wilderness." The *Amplified Bible* says, "Then Jesus, full of and controlled by the Holy Spirit was led." We can clearly see the magnitude of the Spirit's presence in Jesus. We can also see that being full of the Spirit does not guarantee the absence of trials. Believers, when directed by the Holy Spirit, will sometimes be led into a wilderness situation. A wilderness situation may lead to a direct confrontation with the devil, as in Jesus's case. If an individual must have a wilderness experience, however, let him be led there by the Spirit, and let him also be full of the Holy Spirit just as Jesus was.

In the wilderness, Jesus was tempted three times by Satan. Each time He passed the test and was victorious.

A good point to note here is that the Spirit will not lead us into any situation or any place that he will not lead us out. As long as we remain faithful, the Holy Spirit will see us through. Luke 4:14 says, "Jesus returned in the power of the Spirit." He was led of the Spirit into testing, and He returned in the Spirit. When He returned from the wilderness testing in the power of the Spirit, He went to the synagogue and read from Isaiah's writings that which was fulfilled in Himself.

> The Spirit of the Lord is upon me because he hath anointed me.
>
> —Luke 4:18

He walked around full of, anointed with, and directed by the Holy Spirit.

> God anointed Jesus of Nazareth with the Holy Ghost and with power: who went about doing good and healing all that were oppressed of the devil; for God was with him.
>
> —Acts 10:38

Perhaps the well-qualified teachers at Antioch had passed along to the Church what Christ had said to His disciples: "When he, the Spirit of truth, is come, he will guide you into all truth" (John 16:13). In any event, the saints at Antioch were led by the Holy Spirit just as Jesus was. If believers today do not seek for and submit to the Spirit's leadership, we will be blindly groping in darkness and will be unlike Christ as well.

We must be cautious, however, and make sure the Holy Spirit is indeed giving the directions. Although Scripture many times encourages believers to be led by the Spirit, it also admonishes us to carefully discern whether or not the Holy Spirit is indeed the origin of the direction being given. There are many voices of persuasion, but only one voice is truly God. John said, "Beloved, believe not every spirit but try the spirits whether they are of God" (1 John 4:1). By spending time with God in prayer and worship, as the preceding chapter depicted Christ as doing, and by being knowledgeable of the Word of God, we can determine the authenticity of a persuasive voice. The Word of God is inspired by the Spirit of God. Therefore, the Holy Spirit will always teach, guide, and direct in agreement with the written Word. When we present ourselves to the Lord to renew our minds through prayer and communion, we can know and prove the good, acceptable, and perfect will of God (Romans 12:1–2).

In corporate worship, we often hear such suggestions as "Just let the Lord have His way" or "Let's just do however the Lord leads." Both statements sound good, and both are good advice. The sad truth, however, is some who say such things do not truly want God to lead or have His way at all. Instead, they want to do as they please. What they call "the Lord's way" is nothing more than selfish desire that has been formed in fleshly imagination and not in the Spirit. They refuse to accept the fact that God's Word is God's way, and God's Spirit leads according to God's Word. For example, although faithful attendance is scriptural, they think it is acceptable to attend worship services whenever they feel like it. Yet they say they want the Lord to have His way. Although it is God's way for His followers to continually increase their knowledge of His Word, these professors make light of those who study diligently the deeper truths of Scripture. Yet they say they want the Lord to have His way. They do not honor the biblical financial system of tithing. Yet they say they want the Lord to have His way.

The Lord can truly have His way, and the Holy Spirit can truly be chief administrator when believers know and love God's Word. Knowledge of the Word will enable us to test the spirits. We prove our love for God's Word by obeying it and by obeying what the Spirit says to the Church just as the Antioch saints obeyed. We can then humbly say as Christ said to the Father, "Not my will, but thine, be done."

The Early Church Example

The early church followed Christ's supreme example by allowing the Holy Spirit to guide them. They knew they could not perform the duties Christ had commanded without the Spirit's leadership. They were to continue the work of Christ through the enabling power of the Holy Ghost.

The night before His crucifixion, they heard Jesus say, "But when the comforter is come, even the Spirit of truth, he shall testify of me: And ye also shall bear witness" (John 15:26–27). In Jesus's last words, before ascending to the Father, the disciples heard Him say, "But ye shall receive power, after that, the Holy Ghost is come upon you; and ye shall be witnesses unto me" (Acts 1:8). So Jesus said that both the Spirit and the disciples would testify of Him, but the disciples could not do so without the enabling power of the Spirit present in their lives. A study of the early church shows they tarried until they were endued with the Spirit. A few examples will clarify this fact.

In the gospels, Simon Peter seemed the most prominent of the disciples. Although he was well meaning in his actions, he apparently thought he had a handle on every situation. In the early days of the Church, however, Peter had released his grip and had allowed the Spirit to handle both himself and the situation. In Acts 2, he boldly proclaimed the coming of the Spirit as fulfillment of prophecy. In Acts 3, he boldly credited power in the name of Jesus for healing the lame man. In Acts 4, he was called before the Sanhedrin to explain the healing. Verse 8 describes Peter as "filled with the Holy Ghost" as he began his address. He unflinchingly told the Sanhedrin they had rejected Jesus, the only means of salvation.

The importance of the Spirit to the Church at Jerusalem can also be seen in Acts 6. A committee was needed to assure the daily ministration of food was carried out fairly. One of the requirements for doing what was seemingly such a menial task was that the men chosen had to be "full of the Holy Ghost" (Acts 6:3). Perhaps the Church continues to need Spirit-filled, Spirit-directed individuals to hold positions, even if the position does not seem of major importance. Scripture records that two of the men appointed to serve on this seven-man committee of table waiters became able ministers of the gospel.

One of the men chosen was Stephen who, being full of the Holy Ghost, wisdom, faith, and power, "did great wonders and miracles among the people" (Acts 6:8). Resentment arose among the opposition, and Stephen was brought before the council. Although his circumstance was one of persecution, the Word of God says the council "saw his face as it had been the face of an angel" (Acts 6:15). So with face shining under the radiant glow of the Holy Spirit's anointing, Stephen preached one of the most beautiful sermons recorded in the Bible (Acts 7).

One of the accusations Stephen made against those who opposed him was that they were always refusing the very Holy Spirit who was at that time anointing him: "Ye do always resist the Holy Ghost" (Acts 7:51). This was more than they could endure. Like barbarians they "gnashed on him with their teeth" (verse 54). "But he, being full of the Holy Ghost, looked up stedfastly into heaven, and saw the glory of God, and Jesus standing on the right hand of God" (verse 55).

When he began to tell what he saw, the opposition went berserk and started stoning him. But while being martyred for Christ, this Spirit-led man continued talking to God, asking Him to receive his spirit, and to forgive his murderers. The Spirit may lead some to martyrdom, but if so, He will also direct them into the presence of God.

The other man who served on the committee of table waiters was Philip. After Stephen was stoned, Saul led a great assault against the Church, and the Church was scattered abroad. Philip went to Samaria and began a great revival (Acts 8:5–8). Many were saved, and many were delivered from unclean spirits. No doubt, Philip had gone to Samaria by the Spirit's leading because he left when God, through an angel, told him to go elsewhere. Upon obeying, he once again found himself in a situation where someone needed God's messenger. Philip encountered a man in a chariot.

> Then the Spirit [who directed him] said unto Philip, Go near, and join thyself to this chariot.
>
> —Acts 8:29

Philip obeyed and consequently led the man to salvation and baptized him. Here again, Philip was guided by the Spirit, for when they came out of the water, "the Spirit of the Lord caught away Philip" (verse 39).

To be directed by the Spirit should be the aspiration of every believer. No doubt, Spirit-led men of the same spiritual caliber as Stephen and Philip went from Jerusalem to Antioch to begin the Church there. Acts 11:19 says those who did so were "they which were scattered abroad upon the persecution which arose about Stephen." Whoever the pioneers of Antioch were, the church where they were called Christians first was characterized by the practice of being directed by the Holy Spirit.

Another example from the early church is found in Acts 10 when Peter was instructed to go to the house of Cornelius. "The Spirit said unto him, Behold, three men seek thee. Arise, therefore, and get thee down, and go with them, doubting nothing: for I have sent them" (verses 19–20). When Peter reiterated this experience, he said, "The Spirit bade me go with them, nothing doubting" (Acts 11:12).

Peter's obedience resulted in the opening of the door of the gospel to the Gentiles. Shouldn't everyone who professes life in the Spirit also be directed by the Spirit? Wouldn't the Church be much closer to what God has in mind for it if its members sought the Spirit's guidance in every matter?

A strikingly beautiful example of this is found in an action taken by the council of the early church. This action regarded the matter of circumcision as it pertained to the Gentile converts at Antioch. In relating their decision to the Antioch Church, they said, "For it seemed good to the Holy Ghost, and to us" (Acts 15:28). Such an example surely must have had a bearing on the saints at Antioch when they read the letter. Had the early church not continued to be directed by the Holy Spirit, there would have been a break in the chain of continuity from Christ to Antioch where the believers were so much like Christ, they were named after him.

Additional New Testament Examples

Other New Testament examples help show how the church at Jerusalem continued to hand down the Christlike example of walking in the Spirit. The following examples involve Paul, so perhaps it will prove beneficial to review the beginning of his spiritual life. The attitude he displayed at that time is one he pursued vigorously throughout his life. In fact, the attitude believers should have toward the Holy Spirit can be seen in Saul (Paul) at his conversion on the Damascus Road. When he fell to the earth in a personal encounter with the Christ of glory, Saul humbly asked, "Lord, what wilt thou have me to do?" (Acts 9:6).

Just as Saul inquired of Jesus, even so those who are called Christians should often inquire of the Holy Spirit, "What shall I do? What are your plans for me today?" Then upon receiving instruction, believers should obey as did Saul, as did the early church, as did the Antioch Church.

Paul first needed the Spirit's empowerment not long into his first missionary journey. In Acts 13:4, he and Barnabas were "sent forth by the Holy Ghost" with the blessings of the Antioch Church. In Paphos, the third town they visited, they were confronted with a sorcerer and false prophet named Bar-Jesus, who opposed them for the purpose of hindering the gospel.

> Then Saul (who also is called Paul) filled with the Holy Ghost, set his eyes on him.
>
> —Acts 13:9

Paul proceeded to rebuke the false prophet sharply and pronounced temporary blindness upon him. We must remember this was not just Paul, but Paul "filled with the Holy Ghost." Such a powerful demonstration caused the one to whom Paul had been witnessing when the distraction occurred to become a believer.

In Paul's second missionary journey with Silas and Timothy, the Spirit directed where they were to go as well as where they were not to go. In Acts 16, the trio was traveling together on the Asian continent, but they "were forbidden of the Holy Ghost to preach the word in Asia" (verse 6). No explanation was given. Sometimes the Spirit explains, and sometimes He doesn't. The important thing for the believer to do is to obey without explanation. Verse 7 says, "They assayed to go into Bithynia: but the Spirit suffered them not. Again, no explanation was given. The important thing is, Paul and company again adhered to the Spirit's instructions. Later they were enlightened as to why the Spirit chose to bypass Asia at that time (verses 9–10). Paul had a vision of a man in Macedonia asking for help. Assured it was God's will, they went into Macedonia.

From the time of his conversion, Paul was determined to walk where the Spirit directed him. Sometimes the Spirit forewarns of impending dangers. When this happens, a believer's commitment is tested. In Acts 20:22–23, Paul's true commitment was disclosed when he said, "And now, behold, I go bound in the spirit to Jerusalem, not knowing the things that shall befall me there: Save that the Holy Ghost witnesseth in every city, saying that bonds and afflictions abide me." Paul felt he had to go to Jerusalem to remain in God's will even though he knew what the Spirit had said would definitely happen.

Paul wrote, "For as many as are led by the Spirit of God, they are the sons of God" (Romans 8:14). This narrows sonship to the point of being directed by the Holy Spirit in our lives. If Christ was led by the Spirit, then certainly, those who bear His name must pattern after Him.

Holy Spirit Direction

The chief apostle impacted the world with his ministry of Christ. Returning to his home base in Antioch after each missionary journey, he no doubt made a deep impression on the disciples there both by example and instruction. The believers at Antioch were led by the Holy Spirit. They listened to what the Spirit said to the church, and then they obeyed.

To believe in teaching, to practice worship, and to be directed by the Holy Spirit are all characteristics of Christ. He instilled these qualities in the apostles who implemented them in the early church, which in turn passed them on to Antioch. Such Christlike attributes earned them the name "Christians." We who bear the name "Christians" today must also endeavor to be like our namesake.

CHAPTER 8

The Antioch Example: Benevolence

With the rapid pace of the twenty-first century, we easily become self-absorbed. Those around us go unnoticed at times when they are struggling and in dire need of assistance. Such preoccupation is selfish. Unfortunately, this attitude has crept into the circles of those who are called Christians. The lack of benevolence among some who are professing believers is almost frightening.

Webster defines *benevolence* as "an inclination to do good; kindness; a kindly, charitable act." The true church must be and will be a benevolent church. Thus, believers must take heed not to be caught up in the personal pronoun syndrome—"I, me, my, mine, myself." Hebrews 13:16 says, "Do not forget or neglect to do kindness and good, to be generous and distribute and contribute to the needy [of the church as embodiment and proof of fellowship], for such sacrifices are pleasing to God" (*Amplified Bible*). Such charitable actions prevailed in the disciples at Antioch.

The Antioch Example

Only one incident is recorded in Scripture about the benevolence of the Antioch Church, but it speaks clearly of their goodness, kindness, and compassion. Agabus, a prophet from Jerusalem who had come to Antioch, prophesied of a future famine (Acts 11:28). Immediately, the Antioch Church showed consideration for those who were less fortunate than they. Apparently, the church at Jerusalem had become somewhat poverty-stricken by this time, so the believers at Antioch desired to help them. "Then the disciples, every man according to his ability, determined to send relief unto the brethren which dwelt in Judea" (verse 29).

Consider their *unity*—"every man." Comprehending an entire congregation agreeing on anything is difficult. Consider their wisdom in *disbursement*—"according to their ability." No one was made to feel inferior if he had less to give than others. Consider their *resolve and purpose*—"determined to send relief unto the brethren." Galatians 6:10 says, "As we have therefore opportunity, let us do good unto all men, especially unto them who are of the household of faith." Consider also how they *carried out* their resolve—"which also they did, and sent it to the elders" (Acts 11:30). They did what they had resolved to do.

There is no shortage of catalysts in our churches today. Big ideas are plentiful. Starters are usually easy to find. But finishers? Someone to carry out those big ideas? Someone who follows through with his initial resolve? Those people are scarce!

Note also that the Antioch Church was barely out of its infancy. In all probability, it had only been in existence less than two years. Most churches in their early years have their own financial struggles; to think only of themselves and not of others would have been easy to justify. Instead, the Antioch Church voluntarily chose to be benevolent.

Another interesting point is that the Antiochene Christians acted immediately. Sometimes we wait and see if someone who is experiencing difficulty can tough it out and struggle through. We assure people in need we are praying for them when we have at our disposal the very means to supply their need. James 2:15–17 calls this faith without works, which is dead and does not profit. John questioned how the love of God could dwell in those who see their brother in need and have in their possession the means to meet that need but instead close their heart of compassion (1 John 3:17). But the saints at Antioch did not procrastinate, neither did they send a committee to Jerusalem to determine their financial status. When they heard God's prophet under the anointing of the Holy Spirit prophesy about a famine, they made a unanimous decision to be benevolent.

Christ—the Supreme Example

When Peter preached that vitally important message at the house of Cornelius, which opened the door of the gospel to the Gentiles, he referred to Jesus as one "who went about doing good" (Acts 10:38). Doing good is benevolence. Jesus always gave of Himself to others. Benevolence is giving. Jesus was, and is, the supreme example of benevolence.

Christ gave up His royal surroundings in condescending to earth. Philippians 2:5–8 says He "made himself of no reputation" and "took upon Him the form of a servant." He was willing to sacrifice. Benevolence requires sacrifice. In 2 Corinthians 8:9, Paul said of Christ, "He was rich, yet for your sakes, he became poor that ye through his poverty might be rich." He gave up a throne of majesty to come to the lowliness of earth. He gave His life so sinful humanity, from whom He received nothing, could have eternal life. Jesus said, "I lay down my life. I lay it down of myself" (John 10:17–18). In John 10:28, He said, "And I give unto them eternal life." No one has ever given more.

Even when Jesus left the people to rest, and they came searching for Him with many needs, He was compassionate and met their needs (Mark 6:31–34). He taught benevolence in the example of the Good Samaritan who showed kindness to one who had fallen to misfortune and had been ill-treated (Luke 10:30–37). Jesus said it was the duty of humankind to likewise be considerate of others even if it is inconvenient and means sacrificing.

Jesus also gave insight into future judgment in the Parable of the Sheep and Goats (Matthew 25:31–46). Jesus separated the sheep from the goats, setting the sheep on His right hand and the goats on His left. Those on the right inherited the eternal blessings of the Father, and those on the left were cast into hell. The reasons Jesus gave for His judgment were acts of benevolence, those seemingly insignificant things the sheep did for others in need, things the goats neglected to do. Interestingly, those acts were not outstanding deeds but were such acts as providing a meal, a drink, lodging, clothing, a visit.

God sees the smallest acts of benevolence and rewards each one. Jesus said, "Give, and it shall be given unto you" (Luke 6:38). God does not look so much to the magnitude of the gift but to how much we give in proportion to our ability. Jesus said the widow who gave the only two mites she possessed gave more than those who gave in abundance because she gave all she had. The saints at Antioch gave according to their ability. God rewarded them through the spiritual benefits they received from the Church at Jerusalem.

The benevolent acts of God's children will never compare with God's rewards. Just as benevolence can be shown in many ways, God's rewards can likewise come in many ways, none of which are more blissful than the peace and contentment of knowing we have been Christlike.

The Early Church Example

The early church displayed the Christlike attribute of benevolence from the outset. In the early days, they unselfishly shared their resources with others in the church (Acts 2, 4). They sold their land, houses, and possessions and brought the money to the apostles. The money was then distributed to every man according to his need. They "had all things common" (Acts 2:44). This was a most noble and benevolent action on the part of the church, although it probably caused their impoverished plight at the time of Antioch's generosity. Nevertheless, it was a beautiful example of unselfishness, kindness, and love.

Although the entire church was involved in this sacrificial gesture, only one person is mentioned by name—Barnabas (Acts 4:36). In all probability, Barnabas was wealthier than the others, but he still said none of the things he possessed were his own. He was chosen by the church a few years later to observe the mission church at Antioch. Perhaps Barnabas' spirit of benevolence was noticed and imitated by the saints at Antioch. In any event, the early church displayed benevolence and was rewarded with benevolence through the Antioch Church.

Although benevolence is demonstrated in ways other than financial giving, it is closely associated with financial giving. This is the area where many who are called Christians falter. In fact, the first internal problems of the church dealt with finances. Immediately after selling all their possessions and having "all things common," Acts 5 tells of a couple in the church who only pretended to do as the others did. Their heart deceived them, however, and they listened to Satan's cunning voice and kept back part of the price for themselves. Selfishness, like that of Ananias and Sapphira, will become a spiritual sickness. This illustration, titled "Cirrhosis of the Giver," explains it best:

> This disease was discovered in 34 AD by a husband and wife team—Ananias and Sapphira. It is an acute nervous condition which renders the patient's hands immobile when he is called upon to move them in the direction of the billfold or purse and thence to the offering plate. Remedy: The patient may be removed from the environs of the house of God on Sunday since it is clinically observable that the condition does not occur in such surroundings as the golf course, supermarket, or restaurant. A more constructive remedy is to point out to the patient how many income tax deductions may be claimed by overcoming the malady. Of course, the best therapy, and that which leads to a sure and lasting cure, is to get right with God as this affliction is a symptom of a heart need. An old-time preacher once said, "A man's religion never shouts very loud when the mouth of his pocketbook is shut up."

This condition is sometimes excused as "being a good steward over my own house first," but it is truly a heart condition that needs spiritual healing. The following illustrates the proper attitude:

> A man who was in debt for a large sum of money was approached by a friend who said, "Now aren't you sorry you gave so much to the Lord?"

> "No," he said, "I am glad, for that is the only investment I made that is still paying dividends."

Those who are "rich in good works, ready to distribute" are "laying up in store for themselves a good foundation against the time to come that they may lay hold on eternal life" (1 Timothy 6:18–19).

Additional New Testament Examples

In looking at other New Testament examples of benevolence, once again we can see how the supreme example of Christ was handed down. Paul wrote of the benevolence of the churches of Macedonia (2 Corinthians 8:1–5). A collection was received for the poor saints of Jerusalem. Although the Macedonian churches were in deep poverty themselves, they still gave willingly beyond their power. One of these churches was Philippi. Philippians 4:15–16 reveals something of their benevolence: "No church communicated with me as concerning giving and receiving but ye only. For ye sent once and again to my necessity." Paul proceeded to write of their benevolence, and in verse 19 is the familiar promise, "But my God shall supply all your need according to his riches in glory by Christ Jesus." This promise is claimed somewhat loosely today. Doesn't it stand to reason this promise is only to those who do what the Philippians had done?

Paul explained that we reap according to how we sow, then said, "God loveth a cheerful giver" (2 Corinthians 9:7). In verse 8, he revealed the magnitude of the grace of God on the cheerful giver: "And God is able to make all grace abound toward you; that ye, always having all sufficiency in all things, may abound unto every good work."

Paul instructed believers to be "distributing to the necessity of the saints given to hospitality" (Romans 12:13). That was the Antioch way! That is the Christlike way! That is the way for all who are called Christians!

Blessed to Give

The teaching at Antioch surely must have been superb. Apparently, someone had taught them about giving. How else would a church just getting started understand benevolence so early in their Christian lives? No doubt, someone had taught them, "It is more blessed to give than to receive." More importantly, their adoration of God had tuned their spirits with the Holy Spirit, and the love of God shed abroad in their hearts by the Holy Ghost made them eager to give. We are never more Christlike than when we give!

CHAPTER 9

The Antioch Example: Organization

"I'm not going to be brought under any kind of form, law, government, discipline, or doctrine."

Does this sound familiar? Prisons today are overflowing because of such an attitude. The sad thing is, this statement is not made so much by convicts or potential convicts but instead by some who are called Christians. This is the foolish cry of the rebel. This is that all-too-familiar attitude among professing believers who refuse to submit to authority. This pattern of thought causes some to become skeptical of organization as it pertains to the Church. Perhaps a governmental structure evokes a fear in them, a feeling of mistrust or inferiority, causing them to lash out against it to conceal their fear. Most probably, though, it is the renegade spirit of independence that says, "I want to be footloose and fancy free, coming and going as I please, doing my own thing, when and how I want to do it."

Such an attitude has erroneously been called Christian freedom, but it would be more correct to say of such nomadic professors, "They're not free; they're just running wild." Whatever the reason for such a rebellious nature, the bare facts and unadulterated truths are that, throughout God's Word, He has always been a God of organization. Imagine a courtroom without order, military forces without a chain of command, a country without laws or a law-making body or law enforcement officials! "Chaotic" would be a mild description of either situation.

If the business of humankind is carried out by following a structured framework, isn't it even more important that the work of the

Lord be conducted decently and orderly through organization? We don't have to read any further than Genesis 1:2–3 to determine God is not pleased with disorder. When "the earth was without form, and void" and all was dark, God's Spirit moved and brought order and light to a chaotic, dark universe.

God wants His children to have a meaningful existence. This cannot be accomplished if we each follow our own agenda. Doesn't it seem somewhat ironic that some think becoming a Christian means liberty to serve God in a hit-or-miss, play-it-by-ear, come-what-may manner when the very means of securing eternal life for each individual was, and is, based on a divine plan, God's plan of salvation? God himself is an organized planner. He ordains and anoints certain people to certain positions of authority so His plan will be carried out properly.

When people deviate from God's plan, the consequences can be unpleasant. For example, King Saul, on one occasion, decided to carry out the duties of the priest, but he was not a priest. He was told by the prophet of the Lord, "Thy kingdom shall not continue" (1 Samuel 13:14). On another occasion, God's instructions for battle were to destroy every person and animal in the army of the enemy. Saul, however, chose to spare the enemy king and some of the animals. The Lord spoke through Samuel to Saul, "For rebellion is as the sin of witchcraft. Thou has rejected the word of the Lord, and the Lord hath rejected thee from being king over Israel" (1 Samuel 15:23, 26).

If God deals in such a manner with those He has placed in positions of authority, then He certainly wants believers to submit to His plan rather than to insist on their own way of doing things. When God's plan of government and God's appointed representatives are ignored by those who are called Christians, it is indeed a time of spiritual darkness.

One of the darkest periods in the history of Israel was at the end of the book of Judges. Time and time again, Israel had rebelled against God and turned to idols. God allowed them to be brought down by heathen nations and forced to pay tribute to them. Each time God, in His mercy, heard their repentant cries of distress and sent them a deliverer. The last verse of Judges sums up the spiritual condition of the nation during this dark period: "In those days, there was no king in Israel: every man did that which was right in his own eyes" (Judges 21:25).

The church of the Lord Jesus Christ must be organized. In the providence of God, leaders are selected to conduct the government and business of the church. Each leader and each individual member are accountable to comply with and submit to God's Word.

The Antioch Example

The preceding four chapters have revealed a characteristic of the church at Antioch. Just as this amazing young church believed in and practiced teaching, worship, direction by the Holy Spirit, and benevolence, they likewise were advocates of church organization. The Word of God bears witness to this fact (Acts 15:1–2).

A question arose at Antioch about circumcision. Some men had come from Judea to Antioch and told the Gentile believers they could not be saved unless they were circumcised after the law of Moses. This caused some confusion at Antioch. The church wisely elected to send Paul and Barnabas and some other men to Jerusalem to see what church leaders had to say about the matter. This remarkable church recognized the need for church organization. Leadership was needed then, and leadership is needed now to provide an organized way of settling differences and establishing doctrines and decrees.

In Acts 16, Paul and Silas delivered the decrees of the church leaders to the churches, and the churches were strengthened.

> And as they went through the cities, they delivered them the decrees for to keep that were ordained of the apostles and elders, which were at Jerusalem. And so were the churches established in the faith, and increased in number daily.
>
> —Acts 16:4–5

Church government is not a threat to the church but a valuable asset. The church at Antioch displayed tremendous wisdom in referring their situation to church leaders for a decision.

Christ—the Supreme Example

Christ, the supreme example of every good and noble quality, recognizes the necessity of authority and submission. This is verified in various passages of Scripture.

> Lo, I come (in the volume of the book it is written of me) to do they will O God.
>
> —Hebrews 10:7

In John 8:28–29 and 38, He said, "As my Father hath taught me, I speak these things. For I do always those things that please him. I speak that which I have seen with my Father."

Ephesians 4 notes that when Christ ascended to heaven, He gave ministry gifts to us. The gifts were the different categories of ministerial authority: apostles, prophets, evangelists, pastors, and teachers (Ephesians 4:11). The purpose of such God-given organization is important to note because it was "for the perfecting of the saints, for the work of the ministry, for the edifying of the body of Christ" (Ephesians 4:12).

Christ was totally submissive to God's organized plan, according to 1 Corinthians 15:24–28. "Then cometh the end when he shall have delivered up the kingdom to God, even the Father. And when all things shall be subdued unto him, then shall the Son Himself be subject unto Him that put all things under Him, that God may be all in all" (verses 24, 28). To be truly Christlike, believers must be subject to those who are over them. The saints at Antioch, where they were called Christians first, certainly relied on church leaders for guidance.

A look at some of Christ's actions are good examples of just how organized He was. Notice how organized He was when He fed the hungry multitude. He had the people sit in groups of fifty. He prayed a prayer of blessing and thanksgiving to the Father for the food. He then distributed the food to the disciples, who in turn distributed it to the multitude. We usually think only of the miracle of multiplying the loaves and fishes, but remember, this was a hungry multitude of five thousand. When someone is hungry, the animal instinct sometimes manifests itself. But consider this: When a hungry multitude of this size could be fed without utter pandemonium, the distribution was organized.

Jesus likewise displayed His organizational skills at the wedding feast in Cana of Galilee. When told by His mother the wine had run out, He could have caused wine to appear in every empty glass just by saying the word. Instead, He employed a systematic process. "Fill up the waterpots with water," He instructed (John 2:7). After the people obeyed, He told them to let the governor of the feast sample it. In a quiet, organized fashion, He performed His first miracle. Note also that the bridegroom, not Jesus, received praise from the governor of the feast. When we do God's work by following a divinely organized method, we will not always receive the acclaim of men. But which is more important, pleasing the heavenly Father or receiving the praise of man?

At the raising of Lazarus from the dead, Jesus could have been flamboyant and loudly commanded the ground to quake and burst open. Instead, He asked where the body was, told the people to remove the stone, prayed a short prayer to the Father, called Lazarus back to life, and told the people to remove his grave clothes. He carried out the Father's business efficiently.

His organization is also seen when He sent the seventy out to minister in pairs. He did not tell them to go in whatever direction they pleased and to do whatever felt good. He did not advocate ministry in some disoriented fashion. Rather, He sent them out in teams of two with guidelines to govern their ministry. He desired to please His Father. Through His actions, Jesus showed what His Father was like, for "He that hath seen me hath seen the Father" (John 14:9).

Jesus Christ was the most organized individual to have ever lived. Organization was part of His character. To be Christlike, believers must adhere to the organizational structure God has ordained in His

Word. Those precious saints at Antioch realized this was the right thing to do.

The Early Church Example

As in all other characteristics of Christ, the early church set the example of church organization and handed it down as a part of the heritage of the church. Their submission to the authority of Christ was first seen when they returned to Jerusalem to tarry for the promise as He had instructed them to do just before His ascension.

Acts 1:15–23 recounts the organized manner in which they chose Judas's successor. Peter, who was apparently the moderator, said the first reason to choose someone was to fulfill the Scriptures. The successor also was required to have been with them from the beginning of Christ's ministry to His ascension. They then chose two names and prayed that God would show them which one He had chosen. This systematic, methodical handling of church business can be seen throughout the early church. What many fail to understand is that such organized management of church affairs is the result of prayerful, Spirit-directed planning.

Acts 6:1–4 reveals the benefits of church government. In this account, strife had occurred over the daily distribution of food. Remember the animal instinct of a hungry person mentioned earlier? In this particular incident, food was indirectly the reason for the problem. The apostles, those men whom God had ordained to positions of authority, handled the matter most admirably. First, they realized the position in which God had placed them did not warrant them giving priority to this matter personally, so they instructed the church to appoint a committee to handle it. The committee, however, was not just anybody; those serving on it met certain requirements. God's business cannot be conducted in a slipshod manner. The apostles also explained why they wanted a committee to be chosen—so they could keep their priorities in order, both prayer and the Word. Here was organization at its finest, working to the benefit of the church and to the glory of God.

The value of organization is also seen when the church at Jerusalem sent out seasoned veterans of the gospel to assist in new field work. In Acts 8, Philip had gone to Samaria and started a great revival during which many were saved. When church leaders heard about it, they sent Peter and John to them. When they arrived, "They laid hands on them, and they received the Holy Ghost" (Acts 8:17). While they were there, Peter also exposed the true motives of a man who would have eventually disrupted and hindered the work in Samaria.

The important point is, a translocal authority form of government in the church provided leaders to monitor the new churches, to protect them from error, and to disciple them to spiritual maturity. When church leaders heard about the flourishing work in Antioch, they sent Barnabas to them. He encouraged them to "cleave unto the Lord" (Acts 11:23). He took such an interest in the new church that he brought Saul there to help him in discipling the people. This would never have happened without church organization. Christianity is always faced with new challenges and new situations that require doctrinal decisions. These decisions do not need to be made by any one man alone but by an assembly of godly men. This cannot happen without church organization. For example, after Peter first shared the gospel with the Gentiles at the house of Cornelius, the council at Jerusalem was faced with a problem that required making a decision. Although there was contention, the council met and discussed in an orderly fashion the Gentiles receiving the gospel (Acts 11). Likewise, although there was heated argument, the dispute at Antioch over circumcision was discussed in an orderly meeting (Acts 15). The early church always displayed excellency in church government. The saints in Antioch realized how essential organization was to the spiritual well-being of the church. The early church must certainly be acknowledged for setting this example.

Additional New Testament Examples

The early church example of organization and government continued to be handed down throughout the New Testament. Paul wrote to Titus, "For this cause, I left thee in Crete that thou shouldest set in order the things that are wanting, and ordain elders in every city as I had appointed thee" (Titus 1:5). Authority, organization, and sound doctrine are seen here. In 1 Timothy 3:1–13, Paul issued the requirements necessary for men to hold the office of a bishop or deacon. Not just anyone could hold such important positions of authority in church government. Paul also revealed the purpose of such stipulations when he said, "These things write I unto thee that thou mightest know how thou oughtest to behave thyself in the house of God, which is the church of the living God, the pillar and ground of truth" (1 Timothy 3:14–15).

The Word of God has something to say about those who do not advocate church organization. Peter described them this way: "But chiefly them that walk after the flesh in the lust of uncleanness and despise government. Presumptuous are they, self-willed, they are not afraid to speak evil of dignities" (2 Peter 2:10). Jude had this to say about them: "These filthy dreamers defile the flesh, despise dominion, and speak evil of dignities" (Jude 8).

Believers must learn from Scripture the importance of organization, government, and authority, and the respect due those whom God has ordained to conduct His business. Believers must not speak evil of dignities. Believers must not despise government or dominion. Those who do speak evil of dignities and despise authority are labeled "brute beasts" by both Peter and Jude. Let everyone instead follow the Antioch example.

The Nature of Christ

This fascinating church at Antioch saw the need for organization. This can be attributed both to having good instructors and having teachable spirits. Because the saints at Antioch were so much like Jesus, they were first called Christians there. May the nature and spirit of today's followers of Christ be the same.

The Antioch Christians not only believed in teaching, worship, direction by the Holy Spirit, benevolence, and organization, but they also practiced these wonderful attributes. The characteristics of the

Antioch Church are available to everyone. We, as Christians in the twenty-first century, should pursue the Antioch example.

What an honor to be called Christians, to be named after that name above every name!

ABOUT THE AUTHOR

Billy B. Dunbar, the author of *Called Christians*, has been pastor of the congregation at Bethesda Community Fellowship in Russell Springs, Kentucky for thirty-seven years. Pastor Dunbar has a bachelor of science degree in biblical studies from Lee University in Cleveland, Tennessee and a master of arts degree in Church Ministries from Church of God Theological Seminary in Cleveland, Tennessee.

CPSIA information can be obtained
at www.ICGtesting.com
Printed in the USA
LVHW030421140721
692648LV00003B/546

9 781098 094485